GONNAE NO DAE IT

GONNAE NO DAE THAT

(My Writing Life.)

Some Memoirs of
Miller H Caldwell

Matador
Unit E2 Airfield Business Park,
Harrison Road, Market Harborough,
Leicestershire. LE16 7UL
Tel: 0116 2792299
Email: books@troubador.co.uk
Web: www.troubador.co.uk/matador
Twitter: @matadorbooks

ISBN 978 1803137 261

British Library Cataloguing in Publication Data.
A catalogue record for this book is available from the British Library.

Typeset in 12pt Adobe Jenson Pro by Troubador Publishing Ltd, Leicester, UK

Matador is an imprint of Troubador Publishing Ltd

For Fiona and Laura who have heard my tales over the breakfast table, on the beach, in the car, on walks with Tâche and Georgie and at many other places besides, too numerous to tell. They also form a large chunk of my memoirs.

Contents

PREFACE

Gonnae No Dae That

This is a Scots expression imploring someone to stop doing something. The title I have chosen for the book.

Taps-Aff (also Scots Vernacular) Literally 'tops off.' The removing of one's shirt in the event of warm weather. Now an expression describing good times being had.

Taps-Oan, the Antonym: Literally 'tops on' Now an expression describing inclement weather or being down on one's luck.

I owe it to my travels on Dumfries busses where the sign, Gonnae No Dae That is there for all to see. It implores passengers not to speak or distract the driver. This feeling was on my mind as my writing is frequently interrupted by necessary dog walking, shopping, gardening, ironing after putting out the washing and taking it in prematurely if wet or when suitably dry. I don't complain too much. Working from home as she does, in Police secret work, I know it's my wife who brings in the pennies. I began to think of this memoir because life, as it is for everyone, is a matter of interruptions; with many ups and downs. Another factor is the inevitable sand seeping through the glass neck of time, which pushes me towards the book's conclusion. Since the age of 53, over the last 20 years, my life has been as an author. My back-story forms many of the books I have written. That explains why I have so many stories to tell. This memoir shows how these stories have been transfigured into some very unusual books.

I have been a humanitarian worker all of my professional life. I've had significant experiences in Pakistan and Ghana as well as at home in the UK. Mine is an unusual and surprising life. I feel the aches and pains of this new decade make me think that now is the time to write about such influences. I hope this memoir entertains and satisfies you to the point where you see how the jigsaw of my experiences have formed the person I am. Gonnae no dae that. No, I certainly will.

1

Life or Death

I start this memoir at the age of 72. It seems a good time to approach this writing project as I face the inevitable slow progression with a Parkinson's disease diagnosed. At present I have a wobbly right hand that finds new words underlined in red from the keyboard. Yet at times I feel I still have much to offer. Or have I? Has my life made any difference to others? Such questions enter my mind at the very start, because I write this book to show how my books were influenced by my life.

A memoir is about the past. It has to be, it means just that. I remember where I was when 9/11 happened, arriving home to see the incredulous eyes of my daughter and hearing a voice demand that I come and see what was on the television in the lounge at that precise moment, as the twin towers collapsed; and of course when President JF Kennedy was assassinated in Dallas in 1963, I stood in line at a Boys Brigade Friday evening meeting on 22nd November 1963, wondering if I had heard the word 'assassination' correctly; but I do protest when friends suggest I saw Archduke Ferdinand being shot in Sarajevo in 1914 and consequently kick off the First World War. (That I assure you is the longest sentence you will find in this book.) Yet I met men who served in that dastardly First World War. They abounded in Kirriemuir where they attended my father's church. I saw their jingling medals on display on Armistice Day. Kirrie's heroes had no fewer than six Victoria Crosses. I admired their gnarly wooden walking sticks as they sauntered around the wee red Toon. These were men who knew the indiscriminate killings of war, at first hand, but spoke none of it. Serving their country had been their purpose. What then of the generation who missed wars and national service? Was that a perk of being a child of the 50s? Or not?

I was born on 6th October 1950. The early years of what was to become the post war baby boom. Clement Attlee was the prime minister and the local minister was my father.

Small white coffins of children, still numbered prominently in graves, in the immediate aftermath of the Peace, despite the establishment of the NHS two years before. I avoided one white box by the skin of my teeth.

I first saw the light of day at Glasgow's Rotten Row maternity hospital. Not surprisingly, its name didn't

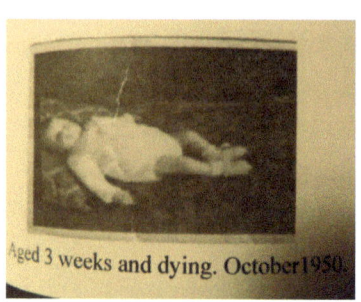

Aged 3 weeks and dying. October 1950.

inspire me to a great start in life. Back at the manse at Bishopton, in Renfrewshire, I was not gaining weight. The local doctor diagnosed a colic which would soon pass. That seemed like an adequate explanation. Nevertheless I continued to lose weight.

The intervention of a medical uncle rushed me to the Sick Children's hospital in Glasgow where I underwent an operation for pyloric stenosis, as they named it then. Now, it's called 'infantile hypertrophy' when food does not reach the stomach. This was the first 'trophy' I would encounter. So, by now, you realise I was a manse bairn. It turned out I was the middle of three manse children; one of whom retains a significant degree of faith and the youngest lives in another world, beyond the grave.

My father, Rev James Caldwell MA moderator of Perth presbytery having just baptised his granddaughter Laura, who became Dr Laura Caldwell, our second daughter.

Of course I knew nothing of my entry into the second Elizabethan age but my second hospital operation was remembered, at the Dundee Royal Infirmary. My father had moved manse to Kirriemuir in county Angus and I was now aged five and a quarter. Fractions play less significance in life as one grows older. But they are

so important to the 5 year old. The operation was so unnecessary. When Joan, my elder sister required her tonsils to be removed for medical reasons, it seemed there was a 'two for one' offer and so my perfectly normal healthy tonsils had the snip too. I was reminded about my Dundee operation when asked to twirl a cotton bud around my tonsils while undergoing a Covid test, more recently. The cotton bud failed to find them, of course.

I was not generally aware of my parents' ministerial frugality. Yet had I looked more closely there were signs. Mum always carried a pair of scissors in her handbag and occasionally snipped some wayward strands of foliage on her urban perambulations, only to see those same stems flourish again in the manse garden. She had green fingers. That was when I realised my parents had considerable control over their growing charges and a keenness to fill the manse glebes with stolen branches.

These early memories had two effects for me. Without my uncle's intervention, I would have died. I realised it was to my uncle, Dr Arthur Stanley Caldwell, Medical Officer of Health for Perthshire and latterly Fife, that I should make something of my life. Secondly, as a manse child, I was a misfit. Living in a large stone Scottish manse had its obvious privileges but provided a very false social structure as well.

2

Bells and Smells

Manse life made its demands on me to conform and to sing. It was the way it was. But what exactly is religion?

Religion is a social-cultural system of designated behaviours and practices, morals, beliefs, worldviews, texts, sanctified places, prophesied ethics, or organisations, which relate humanity to supernatural, transcendental and spiritual elements. It motivates some to serve the Church at home and abroad, for others it advocates terrorism.

However, there is no scholarly consensus over what precisely constitutes a religion. That is perhaps reassuring, if not a relief.

Shortly after turning five years of age I had my first encounter with the spiritual world. A black pastor from Nyasaland, the colonial name for what is now Malawi, whose second largest city is named Blantyre giving it a Scottish flavour, visited the manse in Kirriemuir. (Significantly Kenneth Kaunda, the first black leader of Zambia was the son of Rev David Kaunda an ordained minister of the Church of Scotland. East Africa had many Scottish missionaries.) I digress. In the winter of 1955 this African pastor, as black as the coal in the manse bucket by the roaring fire, came for a pastoral visit to Kirriemuir and stayed at the manse, hugging close to the fireplace on every cold winter's night.

. On Saturday evening, I had my bath but was not ready for bed. I came down to the kitchen where this African pastor was seated in front of the warm glowing fire. His legs were stretched out towards the red hot coals and he had removed his shoes and socks. I sat down beside him and took off my slippers to warm my feet too. It was then that I saw them. His large two feet were not black underneath but white like the soles of my own feet and I told him so. 'Our soles are the same,' I said as I looked up at him. He lowered his hand and rubbed my blond hair with his separated fingers and smiled a magnificent white toothed smile. I was to learn the following morning, in his children's address, that he recalled this encounter and said something about the colour of our skin but we all had the same souls. But in truth I was not following his thoughts. I was still in awe of meeting my first black man. Could this early meeting with an African turn out to be a significant encounter one day?

Kirrie, famous for its East Kilbride made Kirriemuir ginger bread, claims to have the oldest sweet shop, The Star Rock Shop, in Scotland. Who knows, it is perhaps even the oldest sweet shop in the United Kingdom, situated in the town's Roods. The street names were quaint and I became at the age of four, a pupil of the Reform Street School. Education was sedate and comforting. As a 4 and three quarters aged pupil, I sat beside the 12 year old son of a travelling family. Their son, like me, was learning to read. This was a rural school at its best. But after a term or so, he moved on. But I have not forgotten him. This was certainly not a Glasgow city education.

But to Glasgow we went some three years later and from a class of ten pupils, I was in a class of forty five terrified weans. Even before I had a need to clarify why I had been to a Reform street school, I had my work cut out in class. Of one thing, however, I was certain. Long division had not yet arrived in Kirriemuir, before I left, as far as I was aware. I could make neither head nor tail of the puzzle Miss Dick wrote on the blackboard with an instruction to solve it, on my very first day at Shawlands primary school. Solve what? I looked perplexed at the two numbers on a shelf with four numbers under the roof of a straight line. Long division it was apparently named. When her class perambulations led her to my row, she approached me. She saw me place a cross through the equation and give my excuse that I was going to write it out again. Miss Dick decided I required some educational encouragement and holding my ear, brought me out to the front of the class. She lifted her desk drawer and produced a leather strap (aka the 3 tongued Lochgelly belt) and proceeded to thrash me twice.

The pain was excruciating.

My fingers tingled. It was a pain I had never experienced before. I held back my tears, as instinctively I knew each pupil was waiting for my reaction. Neither did it cure long-division instantly, as she had earlier implied it would. Just imagine I was to discover later, a village in which juvenile torture was produced in great quantities, so that every new teacher in Scotland received their Fife Lochgelly leather belt, to utilise at will.

At break I was approached by a pupil named Leslie Hecht showing me some sympathy over my leathering. He asked a most unusual question. 'Was I Jewish?'

I gave this friendly pupil's question some thought. Eventually I recalled that Christ was King of the Jews, according to some sermon I must have heard. So I answered in the affirmative.

'Then bring your yarmulke on Friday morning,' he implored.

'My what?'

'Ah your parents must be reformed Jews. Just bring your school cap.'

Of course I obliged and soon was having Hebrew classes with a new set of friends whose older brothers were having bar mitzvahs and I was invited to them too. There was something rewarding about being a Jew from a manse. Jewish mothers were very loving and provided different yet sumptuous meals. Also, I was taught to sing some Yiddish songs. But a few weeks later my father wondered whether I would be leaning towards a scientific career or more drawn towards the arts. He asked what my favourite subject was. I replied Hebrew was my best subject and his eyebrows flew upwards.

'*Baruch Atah Adonai Eloheim Melekh ha 'olam*,' I said.

'Why are you speaking Hebrew,' asked my father who had studied the subject in his divinity years.

'Because I am a Jew,' I replied.

And these Hebrew words never left me. As a student several years later I flew to the United States on The Camp America's programme. I was selected to go to Pittsfield in Massachusetts, to Camp Onota. That turned out to be a camp for Jewish New York boys. They were impressed by this Scottish Jew's Hebrew until the day we all went skinny dipping at Lake Onota. All was revealed as I stood naked supervising the swimming 'Cubbies'. I was not Jewish after all. The word went out and soon all the camp knew it too.

Cultural experiences continued to make their impressions on me. I also had to keep alert when I was asked to go to Pakistan in 2006 following the South East Asian earthquake. Shalom and Salaam just don't mix. Both describe the same greeting but I only made the mistake once in mixing up the two while I lived in a camp of Sunni Moslems.

It was there I met Osama bin Laden. He came to the Muslim Eye clinic where I was taken to recover from a flu type condition. He called out and I got off my floor mattress and stepped outside to see the tallest man I had ever seen. We greeted each other with a Salaam Alaikum; Alaikum Salaam then he asked of someone I had not heard of, in perfect English. I told him I did not know the man in question and felt my knees give an uncomfortable wobble as I spoke.

'Who are you?' he asked accusingly.

'I am the camp manger at Mundihar,' I told him. 'I am here recovering from flu.'

His eyes seemed to narrow as he stroked his beard.

'Where are you from?' he further enquired.

When I told him I was Scottish he turned smartly and made for the light blue car which had its engine still running.

The car turned left as it departed the compound heading for the next town of Abbotabad. (General Abbot's town, named after him in the colonial days.) On speaking to some victims of the earthquake later, I learned Osama had been seen in the area for some time. I asked if they knew there was a price on his head and all replied that it was payback time for the Americans. Pakistanis would never report him. And they never did.

On my return to the UK I decided to inform my Chief Constable and Member of Parliament that I had met Osama bin Laden in Pakistan. They both told me I must have been mistaken, or demented. They told me he was in a remote cave in the Afghan mountains.

Of course we now know that Osama bin Laden was by then not in a cave. He was living in Abbotabad from 2006. On 2nd May 2011 Osama bin Laden paid the price. He was shot by US Seals, in Abbotabad, and given a nautical burial at sea under strict Islamic laws. I was vindicated at last. I told a few 'I told you so's,' and they apologised. But an extra five years in constant fear of being discovered was an additional burden for Osama bin Laden to bear and I did not grudge him that.

So what did I do when I came back from Africa? Yes, Africa, that's still to be revealed. Well this Presbyterian son of the manse became a school social worker in St Modan's High school in Stirling, a Roman Catholic school. My ecumenical experiences continued.

On Friday nights as pupils set off home, I played indoor football at St Modan's school rather well, in my own opinion. The players were all teachers and Celtic supporters. They forgave my Dundee United allegiances. I was in goal in the gym. It was a soft volley ball that we played with. I got my angles right. I enjoyed those evenings. Less so the work of a school's social worker. I've often wondered if I should have reported my kidnap to the police. It was a significant event with no post traumatic stress counselling on offer in those days. On reflection had I reported the offence, it would do little to enhance the strained relationship between Sean and his angry father.

Sean arrived at the Guidance department's door mid-afternoon on the brink of tears. It was not a school related problem. Sean just feared returning home. So I set off to find out about his family's attitude and response to this situation.

I was met by Sean's father and mother and invited in. I was instructed to circle the room and not go near the centre. Those floorboards were in the fire place heading for ashes. Of course I did not divulge where Sean was instantly and that made his father fly off the handle. He was Sean's father and he wanted his son back in his home now. I refused as I wanted to know how he might be received, what were the bones of contention and how they could be resolved. My agenda was not his. He would not let me leave his house until his son was home. That could not happen. I felt I might have to return to school and seek a place of safety if required for his son. I glanced at my watch. It was 5pm. I would be expected home soon. Then it was 6pm and 7 pm and I was still the unwelcomed guest and prisoner of Sean's father. But then, we made a pact. I would bring his son to his home on the condition that I see Sean at 9 am, the following morning. If he failed to return to school, a place of safely would be sought for his only child. The ground rules were clear. I returned to school, collected Sean from the Guidance department whose staff had remained with him all this time, and took him home, after giving him the reassurances.

That night my wife did not bat an eye when I arrived home at almost 8pm. She thought I was working late.

The following morning Sean arrived at my office with a smile. Whatever the effect, Sean felt it was a warning to his father not to fight with his son again, recognising firmer action on my part would be required next time.

Had the police been involved, a lengthy term of imprisonment could have been Sean's father's fate. That would have done little to cement the fathers – son relationship.

I met the Bishop of Glasgow on 1st March each year, which is St Modan's Day, and Father Fallen from Fallin was the school's chaplain. Every child in the school knew the meaning of alliteration, as a consequence.

The next religion I encountered was when I became the reporter to the children's panels for Kilmarnock and Loudon. One of my Kilmarnock panel members was Robin Wood a leading figure in the Humanist movement. I liked their approach to weddings and funerals and there was a mountain of their pamphlets and leaflets to devour at my leisure. I attended a Humanist gathering back in Stirling and soon felt this religion had many comforting strengths but lacked, for me, a certain confirmation of one's being in the universe.

A twelve year old girl, I shall name Jane, came to her first hearing in the Ayrshire BMK carpet town of Kilmarnock. Her eyes peered over the large wooden and highly varnished table around which sat the reporter, the three panel members, a social worker and the family.

Eileen chaired that hearing and sat immediately opposite the girl. Jane was transfixed by Eileen's figure, a buxom woman with bright red lipstick and matching nail varnish. Eileen was unaware of the girl's fixation with her appearance, as she bent forward to read the statement of facts of the case, while resting her ample cleavage on the table.

'Are they falsies, Miss,' asked the child with an air of naivety.

Eileen drew herself back and responded. 'No, these

are God-given and you one day might have such good fortune to have a shapely bosom too.'

Jane screwed up her eyes. The answer was not what she had expected. She let her know.

'Naw, I meant yer finger nails. Are they falsies?'

Promotion led me south to Ayr, Cumnock and the Doon Valley, while now living in Troon. Another amusing situation comes to mind. One of the panel members came from the beautiful island of Arran. When the last case one afternoon was cancelled, she asked to be driven to Ardrossan where she might just be in time and luck to get the earlier ferry home. I left the case papers in the care of the chairman and set off to the port with Mary.

As we approached the harbour I could see the boat seemed to be departing already. Mary jumped out of the car waving her hands at the boat crew, shouting as she approached the ferry. She didn't want to miss the sailing home. She ran at full pace alongside the ship. Then seeing the outstretched arms of the crewman, she yelled. 'I'm jumping. Catch me.'

'No, haud oan, Mary,' the crewman shouted back at her but her momentum was already flying through the air. He grabbed Mary and pulled her aboard to her obvious relief and delight. She turned to wave to me while the sailor brought her back to earth.

'Yer a damn difficult woman, Mary. We are runnin' late. We've no docked-up yet.'

Further promotion led me to be the principal reporter to the Dumfries and Galloway hearings and then the

Regional reporter becoming the first Authority reporter when the region changed to be an Authority. And our local authority changed with the times.

Dum Gal.com the authority announced. Oops they should quickly change that unfortunate call tag to Dumfries and Galloway.com. Who wants to ring the Council and speak to a dumb gal of a receptionist?

This is a largely rural area with a population of almost 138 million. That is of course, black-faced sheep. Almost 149K people reside within its borders. It's a small region with big intentions. They call it The First in Scotland. It would be equally true, of course, to name it The Last in Scotland when travelling south.

D&G's panel members were Jewish, Baptist, Anglican, Catholic and Presbyterian but it would be wrong to identify them thus and anyway the majority would be undeclared atheists or antagonist, if they themselves knew the difference. It was their Geordie, Lancashire and Lanarkshire as well as Glasgow accents which I heard at hearings indicating the authority's ability to attract outsiders in droves.

Then I took ill with mild cognitive impairment. I could not face a lapsed warrant or neglecting a case for review so I retired at the age of 53, having been a reporter for twenty years. Two years later, the Earthquake struck Pakistan's North West Frontier Province. A local police officer, PC Farooq Ahmed lost his niece in that disaster. I met him in town and knowing I cared for children having been the reporter, asked if I would go out to entertain the children arriving in UNICEF tents at

Mundihar in the NWFP of Pakistan. After discussing this with my wife Jocelyn, I decided, with her approval, to go.

I packed some early reading books, crayons, a mouth organ, glove puppet, paper, string and a couple of balls. I felt able to entertain traumatised children with my distraction of items. No doubt eminent psychologists might have had a different collection in their luggage. But in the end they were hardly needed. I was not destined to be a ventriloquist, story teller, artist, juggler or musician. Except I was asked what the gun-shaped metal object was in my hand luggage at Islamabad airport and gave them a few bars of Beethoven's 9th symphony to prove it was a musical instrument.

It was a Brigadier of the Pakistan Army who appointed me camp manager after an open air January meeting. It was freezing and my hands remained in my trouser pockets to seek some warmth. The matter being discussed was the farm manager's wife who had been suspected of selling and providing aid to local residents, unaffected by the earthquake.

I came to her defence and told the group assembled that the world responded immediately on hearing of an international disaster but organisation, at the point of need, was rarely in position and ready to distribute aid. Then the Brigadier spoke.

'You are not a Muslim.'

I nodded not knowing what else to say.

'You are independent.'

I had to agree with his statement.

'You will be the camp manager.'

I took a moment to take on board what he had just said.

The farmer's wife was incredibly grateful to me as I had saved her from facing a court appearance within a harsh judicial system. She told me so, after the Brigadier had shaken my hand.

I was no longer the entertainer. I was now responsible for 24.5K homeless victims of the Earthquake. This new job would present challenges.

I found resolving disputes in the camp were with loaded Kalashnikovs. Resolving such issues was one of my duties. I was given a Kalashnikov, while now wearing traditional shalwar chemise and a decent growth of beard grew to complement my Pakistani disguise. The tents were aligned around a circular farm hillside. Heavy rain had breached one level and had seeped down to the lower level causing tempers to flare. I arrived to see the damage caused.

'Well, we could stand here all afternoon and as the rain continues to fall we can debate who is in the wrong. Or…' I dragged some mud over the breached area with my shoe, 'or we could assist each other by stemming the flow. At least that is what I believe Kamran translated into Urdu for me but it did the trick. They put down their weapons and got to work.

Flushed with my success, I asked them not to bring their Kalashnikovs to disputes. I did not want any unnecessary funerals, let alone mine.

That reminds me I was also asked to take a funeral in Ghana, West Africa at Teshie, in the south of the country one day. I had some notes in a book of common order and confidently stood by the open grave as the coffin was lowered. Then disaster struck. I had no reference to resolve the predicament which was unfolding before my eyes. The coffin had stuck on its descent. WAWA West Africa Wins Again, the mantra which captures all failed exploits in the country, came to mind. The coffin was lodged at a rakish angle refusing to descend. The grave was not wide enough. I saw the offending and protruding boulder barring the descent and I froze. Should I ask everyone to depart and return when the gravediggers had removed the boulder? Should I simply ask all to stand back and let the gravediggers complete their work? These thoughts were on my mind when an avuncular man dressed in his black funeral cloth approached. He placed his hand on my shoulder.

'I tink we should sing a hymn.'

I nodded my approval and began to think which hymn might be appropriate and would I have to lead them in this cappella performance? But the man had an appropriate suggestion for me.

'I think we should sing, Rock of Ages Cleft for Me.' We sang and the grave opened. Later I would laugh until my sides split at his appropriate hymn for the occasion.

My final denominational encounter was the most pleasant. This Scottish son of a Presbyterian manse married an Anglican. The former Miss France, no less, I add.

Our marriage was in Wigan Parish church, eventually approved by cricketing favourite Rev David Sheppard,

Bishop of Liverpool, as at the time the banns were to be read, I was not English, not a member of the Anglican Church, nor was I in the UK. Vicar Malcolm Forrest required two people to enter marriage. He only had Jocelyn and her word that I existed. David Sheppard not only made it possible for me to be married in Wigan, he also approved my father's part in the marriage ceremony. Father had of course married many brides in the past but to officiate at his daughter-in-law's marriage was a very special occasion for him, in a Lancashire town.

Meeting my first black African pastor was a seminal moment as was the pain of the Lochgelly belt. Being held captive in Stirling's Raploch community should have led to some sort of counselling. I could have benefitted from that. Work in Pakistan and Ghana, led me to a thought that an ecumenical wilderness existed where there is no real God but God could be a vehicle to express the unknown.

Understanding ISLAM

I am not a Moslem although I spent some time in the Islamic State of Pakistan. I lived with many Sunni Moslems and respected their faith. I remain a nominal Christian but my experiences have led me to understand Islam better and I feel I should share these truths.

The Koran was written by human beings at a particular time. A few of its principles are immutable, but very few. Most of the text has to be interpreted afresh by every generation. Thus 'kill them wherever you find them', a phrase about infidels often quoted by fanatical

Muslims and by hostile non-Muslims alike, was written at a particular time of war and referred not to infidels in general but to some of them who had come as spies to betray a new and struggling Muslim society.

It is not the status of the Koran that is the problem, but the minds of its readers. We betray the whole text if we adopt literal interpretations of particular passages. It must always be read in conjunction with the writings that interpret the tradition and the advice of the scholars, and in the light of the prophet's own life and the examples he set. (This much is true of the Old Testament.) Nowhere did he ill-treat women or infidels. He allowed those of his followers who left the faith to depart, unmolested.

Muslims also face many problems today on which their texts are silent. There was no cloning in the prophet's time for example. Faced with such questions, Moslems have to use their minds to formulate new interpretations and principles.

Sharia Law is a way of finding a spiritual path that will make hearts faithful to God in the light of six things, all of which are important. They are: your religion, your personal integrity, your intelligence, your knowledge and intellect, your family relationships and your dignity.

If we meet Muslims taking drugs or committing adultery there is no point telling them that Islam forbids these practices; they already know that. We must understand their psychology and their circumstances before we can move forward.

So how should Moslems respond to dominant groups in the countries where they live? Some try to become invisible. But the opposite is required. Speak out, quote best principles of the society to our fellow citizens. They must claim their rights and fulfil their responsibilities. Work with other faiths to make the schools better for us all and so build trust between us.

The Koran sanctions the death penalty and it is used in 50 out of 55 Muslim states. In six, there is stoning of women. 'But', said Professor Tariq Ramadan grandson of the founder of Egypt's Muslim Brotherhood, 'most of these are corrupt, tyrannical, racist societies where such powers will be used corruptly and tyrannically. So we must say Stop. But Stop, in the name of Muslim values, not in order to please the West'.

Conditions in jail at Guantanamo Bay are appalling, but we should also recognise that they are far worse in Egyptian or Saudi Arabian jails.

In conclusion, if conservative Moslems and the non-Muslim majority in our society will give young people sufficient time and space they will make a contribution to their own communities, the country and western society, for which we will all be grateful.

Our forebears trod the same path. Society changes. Adjustments have to be made.

Each experience was a valuable resource for an author and one which was a colourful background to become a children's reporter.

3

Taps oan first, then Taps aff

Life is never fair. One makes it as comfortable as one can, but many influences can thwart the individual's intentions.

Physical punishment at Shawlands primary school was sore at the time but I got my own back, in a surprising way. Justice was about to satisfy me. Or perhaps it was revenge.

Our family were advised that a golden cocker spaniel from Alyth would be a good idea to join the Caldwell household. I'm not sure who gave the advice. Perhaps it was the farmer who could not get rid of his last puppy. Kirrie was a fine young pup, a good-looker you might even say. That's all it had going for it. It entered the manse and soon adopted a higher than expected pecking order position. First it killed my pet rabbit. Kirrie bit the wire and eased Rodger out of the frame of the hutch. I could not get the image of a terrified rabbit, as the dog entered the hutch with its snarling teeth, out of my mind. The rabbit would have frozen, preparing for its fate. A trail, of blood was on the grass and then I saw the white fur and severed bloody head and Kirrie licking his lips. This image is seared in my memory of some sixty two years ago as if it happened yesterday.

And woe betides anyone who offered to pick up my mother's ball of wool if it was on the carpet. To do so would result is a shark attack from behind the settee. Kirrie always drew blood but was not quite ready to be put down. He had one last attack to make and I'd praise him for it, this time.

At the end of my first traumatic term at Shawlands Primary, there was an end of term church service. Father was the school chaplain. As we pupils shuffled out of the church, eager to begin the summer holidays, I noticed a charming Miss Dick speak to my father. How that woman could change her personality so easily seemed a mystery to me.

And I never thought more about that moment until we were on our annual family holiday at Carradale on the Kintyre peninsula. We were having lunch when it was announced we would be going south to Southend for afternoon tea. Not what I thought was a fun afternoon but father had not finished.

'Miss Dick has invited us to her holiday home.'

Now when a child was strapped it became a secret to every pupil who saw the assault, for that was part of the deceit. It was never revealed to a parent. It would be the first time I defied my parents. I did not budge. I informed them I'd be at the harbour with my fishing line till they came back. Never before had my parents been faced with such a stubborn child but I was certainly not going to afternoon tea with that evil teacher. I stormed out of the house.

I caught nothing that afternoon except a leggy crab. I threw it back into the sea. Shortly before 5pm, I walked slowly back to the holiday home with my tail between my legs. As I approached the cottage the family car passed by and not an eye gazed on mine. I knew I had still to face the music. When we assembled in the hall, I was told to go to my bedroom for my disobedience. That was bearable but Dad, not a keen dog owner, was telling the dog off for being such a bad dog. Kirrie, whose mind had little recall, ignored my father. Strike when the iron is hot when scolding a dog; don't give it a long car drive home and start the discipline. The dog will think you have lost your mind.

My sister appeared at my bedroom and informed me that Kirrie was invited into Miss Dick's immaculate cottage. It was not a holiday cottage, after all, but her second home, soon to be her permanent home on retirement. Kirrie lay down beside my mother on her comfy armchair. In due course Kirrie noticed Miss Dick had left the room and he heard the kettle switch flick

on. Before the arrival of the pot of tea, Miss Dick appeared once more with a plate of strawberry tarts. Six large strawberries sat upon the cream within the short-crust pastry, covered with the red syrup which was known to roll over the pastry lip, on some occasions. With a keen sense of smell Kirrie sat up. I mean he rose up in the poised position of a nuclear armament. Miss Dick placed her hand on the side of the plate and as she offered a strawberry tart to my mother. Kirrie let fly. All could have been forgiven had Kirrie scoffed a tart but instead he felt he was being teased. The plate had been brought close to him then withdrawn. That was not on. In the time it took to blink, Kirrie had launched his long snout at the hand which had offended him. His teeth drew blood, the exact same colour of the strawberry syrup and both began to drip down onto the white polar bear rug beneath them.

I imagined the scene over and over again. I saw the fear in her eyes as the gloom descended; the same gloom when that strap appeared. Then came the pain of the bite; my sting of the taws. Retribution. Taps Aff.

If I thought primary school was tough, so was my secondary school but in a different way. I was sent to Glasgow Academy, not on a scholarship but on a grant for the less remuneratively paid. Ministers aren't well paid. I am sure you are aware of that fact.

In my bookcase beside me as I write this memoir, are books bearing the school motto; prizes for mathematics, general knowledge, French, and physics. It's odd how French gets a capital letter and not physics. There could be little doubt I'd be following the paths of my father and his brothers into dentistry, medicine, veterinary surgery or the church. There was little doubt because these prizes were in my first few years at the school.

There's no need to go into full detail about what happened other than to say, my abuser's mother felt something was awry, and opened his bedroom door with a grunt as the barricading chair toppled onto the carpet. Before her, were two naked males. A mature pupil stood ill at ease. Her son was three years my senior and I stood coyly as an immature me. This was the culmination of a series of grooming incidents from under the Langside railway bridge to the elm tree on Lubnaig Road. What happened left an indelible mark in my life and it started the very next day back at school.

My abuser lived two hundred yards away. During each class I plotted how to get home safely. I'd linger in the centre of town. Boots corner's three floors knew me well. I'd walk to St George's underground station rather than Kelvinbridge station where he'd take the subway. I'd take a bus home getting off a stop earlier or later and the same with the train, getting off at Cathcart or Pollokshaws but never Langside. I simply had to avoid him, at all costs. My subjects began to suffer. That was a mystery to staff and my parents.

My abuser left school and went to study History at Leeds University but that was no relief. He'd be home at Christmas and Easter and those long summer holidays. He lived just one road away. I could not get him out of my mind. I did write about him in my free English essay and got a Higher English grade. It was my only pass that year. Examination markers probably thought it was a fantasy I had written. After all, such things were not talked about in the 60's. Taps Oan most certainly.

I gained enough grades to become a social worker.

To Edinburgh I went to study for three years but during the long summer holidays, I set off to Camp America in the Berkshire Mountains of Massachusetts. The Jewish camp as I mentioned earlier and I felt for the first time, in a very long time, a freedom I could not have imagined before.

I was now a qualified social worker, thinking I could understand cases of child abuse more than most but where would I work? Then I was thinking of applying to the Orkney Council social work department. But I was in Edinburgh's New Town, passing 121 George Street. Somewhat instinctively, I entered and approached the reception desk. Why I had arrived here was a mystery to me at first. It was certainly an unplanned visit. Or was it my encounter with the African pastor in my early years, who was speaking to me? Serendipity? Well, perhaps. But it seemed just right.

'Can I speak to someone from the Overseas Council?' I asked without an appointment of course, but delivered with some appropriate authority.

'A moment please,' the receptionist requested as she lifted her phone.

The wait was significant. It gave me time to absorb the pictures of Africa and missionaries with bibles in hand, striding forth along laterite tracks with the occasional mud house in view. I could not get out of my mind, the black African minister who stayed with us in Kirriemuir. Then her phone was returned to its cradle. She looked at me.

'Rev Neil Bernard is free to speak to you. He's on the third floor.'

I climbed the marble steps counting the floors, passing the hanging pictures of past Moderators of the church. Then I saw the name on the polished wooden door. I knocked.

I was met by Rev Neil Bernard, an avuncular individual with a broad smile. A welcoming gesture indeed though he could not have known my agenda.

'Come sit down,' he gestured with his hand. 'What can I do for you?'

I took a deep breath realising I had no idea how this meeting might conclude. But somehow it seemed right that my footsteps had led to his door.

'I am a qualified social worker. I wondered if the church has an overseas position for me?' I asked seeing in my mind's eye the disappointment of this request in my abuser's ears. And that's all I said. His response was almost alarming. The broadest of smiles passed over his desk. Then a more sombre tone was heard.

'The Biafran civil war in Nigeria is over. But the Igbo tribe still need protection. They are well schooled. They are lawyers, accountants, engineers. Oil is coming ashore from the Rivers state coast of Nigeria and they need the Igbos back to assist in securing the oil riches for the country. There is to be a protected community of Igbos in Port Harcourt. They need someone to run the compound. An outsider would be best. I think you'd fit the bill.'

Africa, like Camp Onota, far from my abuser, wonderful. No, not the island of Orkney but West Africa.

'I'm certainly interested,' I said in a response which

belied my understanding but showed my unexpected gratitude.

'But first, the missionary college. You will go to St Colm's, here in Edinburgh.'

I thought there'd be a catch. Just what would that entail? In fact it turned out to be a most wonderful experience. Morag was a nurse heading for Malawi; Hilary to Ireland; Margaret to the Western Isles; Harry to India; and David to Kenya. We shared in dish washing chores but we had a cook; we had access to washing machines and a tennis court. The Botanical gardens was opposite the college and was where I would be found in late November, trying to acclimatise myself to the humid heat of West Africa.

I did not stay there at weekends. You see, I was not a member of the Church of Scotland. I had rarely been in church since my early teens. If I was to be sent by the church to West Africa, I was required to become a member. That seemed a fair enough deal.

I had needed to get off the bandwagon of Sunday school, senior Sunday school, Boy's Brigade and then communicant's class. I did. I left the BB and left the senior Sunday school with little parental opposition, in fact with no apparent parental resistance worth mentioning. I chose to go to Cathcart church and not my father's in Shawlands and this is where, after six weeks, I was accepted into church membership but on Christmas Eve, I was informed the Rivers State Regional Commissioner in Nigeria had smelt a rat. He would not permit a settlement of Igbos in Port Harcourt citing the civil war was not long past and he did not want to risk it erupting once more. To rub salt into my wound, he marked my passport not with a visa permit but with a stamp shouting loud and clear PERSONA NON GRATA in NIGERIA. But I was told to return to St Colm's in January as I had begun driving lessons, paid for by the church, and a new post was under consideration.

To be honest I'd prefer a driving test on Orkney, even Timbuktu but not Edinburgh. On the day of the test I was doing well. My eyesight had been tested by a car registration about twenty yards away. I think I could even tell the examiner what colour of eyes the driver had. My knowledge of the Highway Code was exemplary. The problem was the weather. The flurries of snow, which were circulating as I arrived at the test centre, increased. It did not seem right a test could be conducted in these wintry conditions. By the time I was crossing the North Bridge, weathermen would have called it a blizzard. We proceeded at a stately and appropriate 18 mph and took a left turn. I was asked to stop the car and duly did. Then I was asked to reverse the car back onto the road from which I had just left. I did so. However as the snow had covered the pavement, the back tyres mounted the hidden kerb. I knew then that I was not only in deep snow but on thin ice as well.

'You are almost there, sir. Your next test will see you through, but not today.'

There is no right of appeal as far as I am aware despite having grounds for consideration but when I returned to the college crestfallen, I was soon thrilled to learn Rev Dr Sintim-Misa had been in Edinburgh and had heard that I was no longer going to Nigeria.

He wanted me as a social worker at the Ghanaian port of Tema, the town which, like the baby elephant, was born big and had eight different communities in total, at that time.

Mission work required me to drive a car. An old large 5 seated Opel was found and so off I went to the Accra airport police station where the inspector pointed his stick at the words 'low flying aircraft' and asked me to read them. Likewise 'No Entry' was another he pointed to as I read the message on the wall chart. My literacy had been tested to perfection and so we progressed to the open road. The peculiar Ghanaian driving test was underway.

I approached a T junction and asked which way he wished me to turn. 'You chose,' he said so I veered towards the centre of the road and flashed my right indicator. It seemed a casual outing with very few instructions. My only concern was I was not familiar with the Accra residential maze of grand houses.

'Make you turn the car around,' was his next command and I duly looked into my rear mirror, slowed to a stop then engaged first gear to complete my three point turn.

'Where are you going?' he asked accusingly, as I engaged reverse.

'I'm making this movement in three stages. I'm at stage two reverse, then drive off in first gear,' I said politely and confidently.

'No, I said make you turn the car around. Just drive over the grass.'

'I did as he bade me and I caught in the corner of my

eye, the residence. It was the residence of His Excellency the Russian Ambassador to Ghana.

The rest of the test continued without even an emergency stop and I realised why with a Ghanaian licence, I would not be permitted to drive in the UK without a British licence.

Six years later, while staying at the manse at Abernethy, I drove to the driving test centre at Cupar in Fife having first stopped at a garage to find some L plates. My International Driving Licence was still valid but nearing its expiration date. It did however, explain to the examiner how I was able to arrive unaccompanied to his test centre.

Cupar is a rural Fife town and on the outskirts are some rather fine stone buildings where the good and wealthy live. I was approaching a slow curving bend, in that vicinity, where the end of the 30 mph sign appeared beyond a road entry. A car appeared from that opening and seeing me approach the end of the 30mph zone at a modest 24 mph assumed my slow speed meant I was going to turn into the road from which she was leaving. Her conclusion was ill advised. As I approached where she was, she engaged first gear and moved straight into the path I was travelling. I applied the emergency break and brought the car to a skidding standstill.

'Handbrake on,' the examiner ordered and he proceeded to leave the car. He remonstrated with the driver almost bringing her to tears. I could hear most of the words he shouted being, 'Test Driver had the right of way, you require to re-sit your test.'

He returned to the car and secured his seatbelt. 'We

can return to the test centre now. I will not be giving you an emergency break instruction.' And so I sat my driving test three times, failed once and passed twice. That's a conundrum I reveal when social intercourse sometimes stalls.

But that is not the end of the story of this chapter. Flight from my abuser to Africa was reassuring, yes comforting. It was a real escape. And you will recall how Ricky gave Miss Dick her comeuppance? Well, when I was sixty five, I wrote about my abuse in the book, A Lingering Crime. It focussed on the circumstantial evidence of sexual abuse. That of itself was unusual. There was the escape, the secrecy, the continuing fear, the impact in choosing a career. Circumstantial evidence too had also to be stressed and given credence in court cases. I experienced all these facets of abuse.

It was a book which had early success. At the Scottish Association for the Study of Offending annual conference at Cumbernauld, it sold well; its only negative review pointed out a couple of spelling mistakes in this self published book. I carried on writing and published several books after this one. In truth A Lingering Crime had gone right out of my mind.

Then in early 2021, in the middle of the Covid 18 epidemic, I received an e-mail. It came from Los Angles where Daniel Guardino was a successful film script writer. (Heart Stopper and My Own Worst Enemy are two of his successful films.) He had come across my book's title and bought the book. Now he wanted to make it a film script. Of course, I gave my permission.

In fact not only do I now have his film script, Daniel has sent it to Fulfilment Pictures. My abuse heading to be a film?

TAPS AFF indeed, at last.

4

WEST AFRICA WAWA – West Africa Wins Again

West Africa has a special part in my heart. It's where I found romance, enjoyed the work and made many Ghanaian lives better though health and employment projects. This was the continent I first heard about and experienced in the manse at Kirrie fifteen years before. West Africa has featured in several of my novels.

To some I was the Scottish missionary at Tema. But I never used that title. I was a fraternal worker. It was a less presumptuous title and one more appropriate for this era. Arriving in Ghana in February 1973, sixteen years after The Gold Coast acquired its independence, I could take a cynical view as my salary arrived in sterling in Accra and was dished out to me in Ghanaian cedis when I needed some. Two years later the church auditor received a prison sentence for stealing my sterling and the salaries of other Scottish missionaries.

I was asked to preach, play the organ, take funerals, and lead a youth group. In doing so I realised Ghanaians had a deep understanding of their faith during daylight hours but in the evenings they often attended the spiritual church groups. A double insurance policy, I assumed.

After my first tour of duty; two years in the white man's grave of West Africa; it's three years in India; my life changed dramatically. It occurred when I least expected it to. Indeed I had told my parents as I set off once more on my second tour of duty in Ghana that

marriage was not my thing, just not for me.

But I should also reveal and admit I was in bed with another woman soon after my parental admission of celibacy.

As I planned my second tour of duty, I had some international flight experience. I fancied flying to Cairo for an overnight stop and then on to Ghana. I informed the church who approved my plan as it was a cheaper fare they were paying. My first tour had been from Paris to Abidjan, in the Ivory Coast, then Accra on a UTA flight.

This time I arrived at Cairo in the dark. Not just night-time darkness but war conditions prevailed. Israel was at war with Egypt and the airport was in almost total darkness.

I was given a key to room 6 and was directed to a low row of buildings. As I approached I was able to make out that this was the airport's overnight accommodation for transit passengers. No lights were on in any of the rooms. I counted along the veranda. The door of room six was slightly ajar. I entered. As my eyes adjusted to the unlit room I was aware of a movement in the bed. I froze. The voice spoke.

'Who are you?' an American black woman asked as she sat up in bed.

'I'm dreadfully sorry. I have room 6. Here's my ticket, 'I said showing her the chitty from a position she could not possibly read. But she was convinced it was accurate.

'Guess they've made an arse of it. Here, get in your side of the bed, and by the way, no hanky panky. You hear?'

I nodded my reply, stupefied to the core. With armed soldiers parading around the forecourt, I had no intention of walking out again. And her strong warning that I should not engage in any hanky panky, implied it would be an uneventful, but restful night. I prepared for bed and entered the covers. Before I fell asleep, a thought came to my mind. What was I doing in this missionary position?

In the morning, I pretended to sleep on as she dressed. Then she told me she was heading to Nigeria to try and trace her ancestors, her native roots. I wished her luck. When I told her the work I was returning to do, she laughed.

'In bed with a missionary, that's a first for me.'

I laughed quietly. 'And a first for me too,' I added unnecessarily and then she was gone. I never even asked her name for it would still have been remembered to this day. Before I left the room I looked again at my ticket. Indeed it was for room 6 but when I turned it around it suggested 9. Oh dear.

How people meet and fall in love these days requires a computer. A matching service begins. Make a date if you like who you see or was it the voice on the zoom? Our romance was less automated; yet more complicated. Jocelyn walked into my life quite unexpectedly. Her housemate in Bekwai in the Ashanti region of the country had received a letter from Inverness. Jennifer's friend told her she had met the Tema fraternal worker when he came to speak to her church in the north of Scotland, on his furlough. So Jennifer, a maths teacher and Jocelyn a chemistry teacher, brought some twenty students to Tema Secondary school to live, while during the day they toured the Industrial parts of Tema. Jennifer just had to meet this eligible Scot. At least that was what I took from the letter I read on my return to the town. Both girls were going to visit me and I made sure there was a chocolate drink handy for their evening nourishment.

To be honest I was instantly smitten by Jocelyn but as a Wigan Lancashire Lass, she could not compete with the central Scottish contacts and experiences Jennifer and I shared. Romance was slipping from my hands. I suggested they returned the following night when I would have a meal ready for them and of course, I had time to prepare my opening gambits with Jocelyn. That was on my mind as I struggled in this new romantic territory. In fact, what was about to happen was a total nightmare and an almighty disaster.

I had a cook steward but he left to work in the harbour as a crane driver. So, as not to let me down, he had arranged for his cousin to come to cook and wash for me. She had her City and Guilds domestic service certificate. Her name was Rejoice and an apt name it was.

I went to the Tema Secondary school in my red slouch-backed Opel Ascona sports car to collect the girls. (A present from the German Presbyterian church no less, who knew just what a young missionary required to fulfil his motoring engagements.)

When we entered my bungalow I heard the shower was engaged. No sign of Rejoice but I put one and one together. It was the very first time she had used the shower in my home. A few moments later Rejoice entered the lounge as I was speaking to the girls. She knelt down beside me with an exposed bra-less black back for me to zip her dress up. Now, I had been asked to fulfil this function on some occasions in my manse days with my sister and mother so I knew what to do. I zipped her dress up to the nape of her neck without deviating from what I was discussing but I was to learn later that it gave both girls a very uneasy moment and a moment to reassess this bachelor missionary's behaviour.

It was a fish tail dress she wore. A very fashionable tight fitting dress with fanned out fins at her feet and hence the name. Rejoice made her way to the kitchen.

Prior to eating I brought out my guitar and we sang a few Glasgow street songs. That was another mistake. Jennifer knew these catchy songs but Jocelyn just had to bear me out, as my singing Glaswegian accent elongated the vowels.

I simply cannot think what we had to eat. Chicken fufu perhaps or rice and Okra stew? Infatuation made me eat even less and I thought Jocelyn was in a similar vein. No matter how I tried to enter Jocelyn's world, I was doomed. 'Ah you come from Wigan,' I said feeling neither rugby league's Eddie Warring nor the Wigan bump fad were appropriate social starters.

'Yes, I'm from Wigan in Lancashire,' she said.

'Fascinating,' I replied and the moment had gone.

Then it happened. A voice started to repeat itself calling out 'Jennifer, Jennifer, Jennifer.' The sound came from just outside the window that night, from the cage where I kept Kofi, my African Grey parrot.

The previous night after the girls had returned to their Tema school accommodation, I had consoled myself stroking the parrot's neck. As I did so I thought it would be fun for the parrot to assist in my romance by calling out Jocelyn's name the following night.

'That was Jennifer and Jocelyn, Kofi. You hear me, Jennifer and Jocelyn,' I told the parrot that night as Aruna the night watchman looked on.

The parrot cocked his head. 'Jennifer,' it replied.

'Yes, but I want you to say Jocelyn,' I instructed the head bowed bird.

'Jennifer.'

'No, Jocelyn. Jocelyn, Jocelyn.'

The following night Kofi reverted to his favourite new word. 'Jenifer, Jennifer,' it shouted at the top of his voice and Jennifer smiled at me while Jocelyn felt I had made my intentions very clear.

I returned the girls to Tema Secondary school on the final night, feeling dejected having let this beautiful girl slip out of my life, with the parrot aiding and abetting me to do so. Then surprisingly, things turned around.

Jocelyn loitered by the car as Jennifer mounted the

school, steps. She turned towards me and informed me that her brother was visiting her, in Ghana, in two weeks time.

'Gavin flies in on the Saturday morning from London, …very early…I was wondering…could I possibly come …to Tema…on the Friday night and could you come with me to collect him at Kotoka airport the following morning?'

By the time Saturday morning broke, we were holding hands and both of us knew this was a special friendship.

Indeed it was. As I write this book, we have been married for forty five years. Taps Aff indeed.

General Ignatius Acheampong was the county's ruler and when we left six years later, he was publically executed on Labadi beach for corrupting the country's economy. One of his great disasters was Operation Feed Yourself. On paper it was a good idea but in reality it drove young men from their villages into arid areas where they were given no agricultural implements to work the soil. The army visited these sites and with their sticks beat those who were not working hard enough. Taps Oan.

I met with them bringing food and extra clothing from the COP (Community Organisation Project) funded by the council of churches. I also secured employment at the Rubber estate in the far-east of the country at a site where a bad tempered German national ran the show. He made no secret of his father's Nazi SS past. At first he doubted I had eighteen willing workers but after a year, he changed his tune. They were well fed, well paid with enough money to send back home to their families. To thank me, I received a small monkey whose mother had been shot by a poisoned dart. The monkey was totally dependent on us and we bonded with him immediately.

I also got a work party to clear the drains of Ashaiman. This area was where the poorest residents of Tema's communities lived, in squalor. Weaving through their aluminium roof and mud walls, flowed the stench and putrid smell of decaying fish and human waste. It was an area which spread disease as easily as the wind blew the palms. But it was cleared. With local nurses and local politicians to educate, their standards were raised and fewer fell ill.

We can expect a meal when we are patients in hospitals in the UK and I must recall some very tasty meals in Crosshouse and Dumfries hospitals. In much of the third world, relatives are expected to feed their patients.

Our Community Organisation Project bought the land around the hospital and a happy band got to work to plant tomatoes, onions, garlic, cassava, plantain and banana. (Plantain is similar to banana except one is a fruit, the other is a vegetable. When in growth, the plantain fingers stand erect while the banana's fingers flop downwards.) Good to learn one thing a day, not so?

My work in Ghana was not particularly evangelical. It was practical, it was needed and it was humanitarian. I had also restrained all my sexual urges in such compromising positions. It turned out to be a precursor to a real loving relationship.

5

This Sporting Life

I have always enjoyed sport, playing it and increasingly watching it on TV these days. Match of the Day on Saturday nights, Wimbledon fortnight and the home countries rugby internationals now but in my day, well, I gained two International caps and played for the German football national team. Or did I? Well, let me explain.

My first encounter with sport was football. No, not a team player. I was not yet a school pupil so I must have been aged four. I played alone in the lane between the manse and Church knowing that the church is one sure foundation, the ball would not damage the edifice. That was despite its softer red sandstone material. The ball required a dubbin finish every so often to bring back its leathery shine and it had to be inflated from time to time, as well. But the game ended abruptly after six weeks or so.

This picture shows the route of the lorry. It would have slowed down to turn. I played where the car is situated, the manse back door being just beyond on the left.

I had not taken account of the angles required in passing a ball, let alone receive it, after it had struck the base of the church.

One day I got the angle terribly wrong. Instead of the ball returning to be kicked again at the building, the angle it chose was a dangerous one. It seemed like the ball was travelling in slow motion and the Angus Milling Company lorry was moving at a greater speed. The two would surely not meet. But they did with one almighty bang. It must have disturbed the town citizens and frightened if not terrified the war veterans who must have heard the explosion that day.

I never received a real football again, thus ending any possibility of me playing for Arsenal, and Scotland in the World Cup. But I apparently did play as a German national football team member as you will soon discover. Meanwhile playing for Arsenal and Scotland were regular fixtures for me, when I was entering rapid eye movement as I dreamt.

Rugby was the game at secondary school I played. Of course playtime involved a game of football with a tennis ball in the playground, but it was not a formal school sport. Anniesland was the venue of our home rugby games. I was always going to be scrum material but not in the front row. A flanker they called me in those days. The ones who flew off the pack and tackled the opposition if it gained the ball. If we won the ball then I'd disengage and move forward in case the wingers decided to return the ball back to where the disintegrating pack were located. I admired the swift footwork of the backs William R Shankland and Angus Robertson who were particularly fast and hence regular try scorers. But I grew sufficiently to be a target in the line-outs as well.

Games were between Glasgow Schools, Edinburgh schools and others at Dollar and Helensburgh and around the central belt of Scotland. As I progressed up the school, I moved from the 5th to 4th and eventually to the 2nd fifteen. Then crash. Down I came and I knew I had broken my arm. In fact it wasn't my arm. It was my scaphoid bone in my wrist. Not a simple fracture. The peculiarity of its blood supply is the primary reason for its prolonged healing period. Whereas other fractures in the upper extremity require an average of six weeks, a scaphoid fracture requires an average of 12 weeks if treated immediately.

I was a choir member and had been in the gentlemen's chorus each Christmas pantomime. But in my final year I had the lead role as Dick Whittington in the annual pantomime and so at each rehearsal I was asked when the plaster would come off. It came off two weeks before the first curtain rose but was still in a long cotton bandage. That was eventually removed and the performance showed no sign of an injured Dick. Opps, I mean an injured Dick Whittington.

As an Edinburgh student it was the small white ball I hit around Gullane and the many city golf courses. Nothing of note was achieved on the golf courses in the east so I draw a veil over my performances there. Greater success was on its way.

Günther Netzer played in the winning German UEFA championships in 1972 and was a team member of the 1974 World Cup. This was the pinnacle of his football career and an appropriate time to retire from the game. He played his last competitive match at the World Cup in 1974.

It was rumoured that Günter Netzer had come to Accra to start his coaching career with the Accra based Hearts of Oak football team. But after arriving he had not been seen. A further rumour was that he had suffered the galloping gut-rot symptoms of the tropics and was holed up in the Ambassador hotel, in Accra. With such a delicate condition to endure, the papers had respectfully let him recover in his own good time. But there was excitement in the ranks of Hearts of Oak supporters who were anxious to see this German international footballer bring his magic to the local team.

After dark, one mid-week night, I heard the greeting of 'Agooo?' outside my bungalow. Visitors in Ghana do not knock on the door; they call out 'Agooo'. Then the house dwellers know it's not the knock associated with the more common goat, kicking at the front door. The response is 'Ameee' which I gave as I went to open the door.

Before me was a youth of around eighteen years of age. He was well dressed wearing a clean and bright Jeromi shirt. I invited him in.

The conversation began in a sticky manner.

'You are Scottish?' he asked accusingly. I could not deny that.

'Then you play football?' he enquired further.

'I have played football but rugby is really my game,' I replied. His eyes fell to the linoleum flooring.

'But you know how to play football?' he asked as he raised his head in anticipation.

I still could not follow his purpose in arriving after dark to ask these mundane sporting questions. I acknowledged my knowledge of football with the nod of my head.

'I play for Tema and we have a match against East Accra on Saturday. Can you come to the match?'

I went over to the table and opened my diary. Saturday was free I told him. I'd come along to watch.

'Oh no,' he said with enlarged eyes and a worried look on his face. 'We'd like you to play for us.'

I was worried. I had no idea at what standard they played. Had they the same strip and did they play in boots or bare feet?

He would drop by before the game with a kit, as he said and I could let him know if it was not the right size.

On Friday, when I was out, the day before the match, a bag was awaiting my arrival home. It contained a freshly ironed black and white shirt, black shorts, red socks and a pair of boots, or cleats as he called them in the American way. (Think St Mirren FC for the effect.)

I tried them on and I must say he had got my size down to a tee. The black and white striped shirt was a good size and the black shorts comfortable, showing considerable thigh. The red socks fitted and I felt I looked quite sporty in the colours of team Tema. I recall dreaming of scoring goals then I broke into a sweat as I realised they were likely to be fitter and probably had more skills than I had. It was a restless night.

The following morning I told the occupants of the compound where I lived, about being called up to play for Tema against East Accra. They pounded my back and offered their best wishes for a Tema victory. I told them I was a little scared. But I took comfort in that it was only East Accra and not the whole of Accra, I would be facing.

A team bus arrived shortly after 1 a.m. and set off to the Osu RE playing field. (Osu is a district of east Accra where in Colonial days the Royal Engineers were based. Hence Osu RE.)

We were ushered into a school classroom to change. The opposition were two classrooms away. One of our team listened with his hands cupped to the classroom wall but whether he heard any plan emerge from the opponents, I'd never know. Perhaps the opposition were doing the same thing. But I had an additional problem. The captain spoke Ga fluently and I was an Akan Twi speaker.

We took to the pitch and I was given a forward position after telling them I'd not be good in defence or in goal. Many of them thought that funny. I was not sure why.

A winger whose surname I recall was Quarshi, a Ga and a divinity student at Legon university, in the sixth minute ran down the wing, evading tackles. I was impressed with his flight of foot and hauled myself forward. As he approached the corner flag he looked up. I even thought he was looking at me. Then he crossed the ball and it approached the penalty spot at a good height. The goal keeper stood poised in the middle of the goal having no confidence to grab the ball and clear his lines. I ran a few steps forward and the ball hit the side of my head and went flying into the top corner of the goal, shivering the net as it descended to the ground. I had scored a goal. I went to Quashi and shook his hand. 'A wonderful cross, just perfect,' I heard myself say as a din started around the field. I looked up and saw hoards of youngsters arrive from the capital. One thing only was on their minds. It seemed Günther Netzer was no longer in the hotel, he had recovered and come to this game and what's more in the opening few minutes he had scored a goal. The white man in the team, most surely Günther, had arrived to spread his magic.

Like ants they descended onto the pitch. Every one chanted only one thing as they crowded around me and thumped my back.

'Günta'
'Günta'
'Günta Netzer'
'Günta'
'Gunta'
'Gunta Netzer.'

I noticed they came from the opposing team support to congratulate me, as well. Clearly Günter's presence was a much greater story than the match between Tema and East Accra. The chants grew louder attracting Ghanaian football fans, from further away, to the pitch. When they arrived they saw everyone was around the white man. Their Günther had arrived. Hearts of Oak would soon benefit from his experience and commitment. The club would rise from third position in the Ghanaian league. But the truth was I spoke no German and it was an amazing case of mistaken identity.

The game was abandoned and the local Accra minister who had come to see the game came to my rescue and took me to the Kuku hill manse.

Perhaps you can see why Ghanaians mistook this World Cup winning German forward in 1974 for myself, the long locked, parrot-loving, blond Scottish missionary.

I met a Welshman in Accra, quite by accident. I had gone to Barclay's bank to deliver a letter for the pastor's daughter who worked there and who lived next door to me. It was when I was speaking to Betty Swankier that this man passed by and introduced himself as the manager. His Welsh accent was unmistakable as he tried to ascertain where my accent came from.

'You are Scottish aren't you?' he finally asked.

'Yes, I replied.'

'Do you play rugby?'

I was taken aback as this conversation had taken a definite swerve.

'Er… yes, at school in Glasgow. I was a wing forward,'

'Great. Want to play a game?'

'Er… a game of rugby in Ghana?' I asked incredulously.

He informed me he was a friend of a Ghanaian Army officer who had been to Sandhurst Army School in England and was smitten by the game. He hoped to form an army team and had got Glyn Davies, the Barclay's manger to find some expat rugby players to augment the team.

The team assembled at the University of Ghana sports fields at Legon. And we played on grass, not red laterite grit. So each Saturday afternoon I was found playing rugby in front of Ghana's great seat of learning. What surprised the forwards, men of non-commissioned ranks, was that I spoke Akan Twi. I would give the order to release the ball and as if the request had come from an Army officer, the ball would appear and then fed to the scrum half who was Glyn and he launched the fast backs and tries were scored.

We enjoyed Tata and Guilder beers afterwards and

a spirit of camaraderie was afoot till one Saturday before we started our practice game, the Brigadier told us he had some news for us. We would hear what he had to say at the end of our exertions. In rucks and mauls we heard suggestions that this might be our last game, or the soldiers would be going on a training mission up country, but such thoughts were wide of the mark.

We gathered around in a circle and sat down. The Brigadier stood in the middle and turned round constantly when he spoke. He informed us that in Lagos, Nigeria and in Freetown, Sierra Leone, there were similar attempts to raise rugby clubs. We nodded our approval. Then came the bombshell.

'I have invited the team from Freetown to play us here and two weeks later we will play Lagos. Home advantage is on our side.'

Voices of excited approval were heard. But more was to follow.

'These are independent countries we are playing and so they will be recorded for posterity that these are the first Rugby Internationals you will be playing.'

But who would be playing? I raised my hand. 'Would it be an all Ghanaian national side that plays these teams?'

The Brigadier was quick to scoff that idea. 'The team will be a Ghanaian team. And you play as a Ghanaian when you play here not as Welshmen or as a Scot. We are all Ghanaians. You understand?'

I need not bore you with the details of these international matches except for two matters. We won both games.

Against Sierra Leone we won 24- 5 and Nigeria 19-12. But I did not see the end of the Nigerian match. I was carried off the field with a broken arm and driven to the Military hospital where I was encased in a plaster stookie. (Stookie – a Scots word for a plaster of Paris encasement.) The very next day, sporting my arm's plaster in a sling, Jocelyn drove me back to the Military hospital in Accra where I had been asked to preach a sermon that Sunday morning.

In all these sporting moments, I was a team member. People's problems were solved by people who brought to the table their skills and abilities and that made things work. Humanitarian work can be difficult and tiring but sport lubricates the mind and body to make things happen.

When we arrived in Dumfries, in 1992, friends announced they played badminton at the village of Kirkpatrick Durham near Castle Douglas. What had been a church was now the community hall and marked out on the wooden floor were the lines of a badminton court. I enjoyed my years there, playing with unusual skills playing the shuttle from behind my back, between my legs and frequently sending the feathers to nestle on top of the net. Sometimes it wobbled over to score and at other times, fell drunkenly on my own side and thus I lost a point.

But the badminton club also had summer walks around the beautiful countryside and sometimes further afield in Cumbria and on Arran; a Hogmanay gathering at a restaurant and a meal out on the profits I made as treasurer of the club, once a year. Covid 18 and Alan and Margaret Nicolson leaving Dumfries to head for Hamilton, as well as my rheumatism in my left leg, and now Parkinson's disease, has resulted in a tardy return to play. But I'm still the purse-holding treasurer and we still have funds to spend some time for a meal.

I have not mentioned swimming. You might even conclude it is taken for granted that I do. But why should this be? My feet are not webbed and my nose not meant to be under water. No, I've never really taken to water. I was shamed at not being able to swim at school; frightened by the swimming coach that I threw myself into the water and began to swim. You see summer holidays for me were with my grandmother at Fairlie on the chilly Ayrshire coast. Class mates were on the Costa del something or the French Med as they called it. Warm water places they were. While year after year we went to Fairlie but it was always enjoyable to build sandcastles on the beach. Eventually I'd enter the water and after a few minutes standing up to my waist, retreat for what we called a chittery bite. A towel rub down was maternally provided and a biscuit to follow and my swimming for the year was over.

That should have been a warning but both daughters not only became swimmers with no fear, they dived during their gap years and Fiona, who is scared of spiders in her bedroom, took holiday makers to the Great barrier reef in Australia and then took them down into the deep and instructed them on the different types of sharks. Confident swimmers and divers they are but God knows who they took that from.

We had a family holiday on Corsica not so long ago. We went out on a diving boat with the girls and they were soon equipped with skins and tanks on their backs. On instruction they sat on the rim of the boat (I'm sure there's a nautical term for the side of the boat) then they flopped backwards into the water. Gracefully I might add. Meanwhile the instructor recognised a non diver in me. She suggested I snorkelled around the boat. Glad to be included in this afternoon activity, I struggled to get into this wet suit. Maybe it was a dry suit. I'm not sure of the difference.

It was a tight fit. Then Jocelyn came to my rescue. She informed me that I was placing my left arthritic leg into the arm sleeve!

However that was soon sorted and I made my way with my snorkel in place to the side of the boat. I leant back and did what the girls had done so effortlessly a few

minutes before. But as I entered the water, water started to fill my nostrils and I spluttered.

Coughing and flapping with Jocelyn telling me to use my flippers. That meant floating on my back increasing the water down my nose. Many had drowned down through the ages and I felt sure this would be my ending

too. Anyway completely exhausted with my efforts I eventually got to the rear of the boat and held the rail to recover. Then I was able to mount the steps back to the deck.

I have never swum since nor do I intend to again. I should have listened to my inner voice all those years ago. Water and I do not mix. I only shower these days. Never a bath. Immersion brings back some bad memories. Also I admit these Parkinson's days; I lollop around in a bath unable to get out, as the water cools. Jocelyn knows what to do.

My immediate future, post Africa, was determined by that game of rugby. It was after our international rugby as we continued to play at Legon. A white man stood on the touchline throughout the game and when the final whistle was blown and I came off the pitch, he congratulated me on a fine game. Wondering who he might be, I stopped and engaged in conversation. He asked what I did in Ghana and I told him about being the secretary of the council of churches; on the board of the Community Organisation Project and chair of the Youth Committee. But I had indigenised many of the posts I held and it would be time to return home within the year, I informed him. He asked what I'd do on my return home to the UK and I then stuttered a reply, reluctant to state confidently that I'd return to social work. He saw his opportunity

He explained he was Professor Humphrey J Fisher of the School of Oriental and African Studies, at London University. He felt I had a significant breadth of current

African knowledge and so offered me a place, there and then at the university to study for a year for the post graduate MA in African studies. I hesitated.

'I hold a certificate in social work and the diploma from Tavistock House in social work. Neither of these qualifications were a first degree,' I admitted. So a post -graduate offer was kindly turned down. I felt his offer was a bridge too far for me.

He shook his head. 'Your experiences and work in Africa over six years is more than a first degree. The Masters is a one year course of study, you will enjoy it,' he responded.

My cards had been played and he had come back with his final offer. Only one year I realised and if I applied myself, a post graduate degree as well. I accepted his offer, returned home and told Jocelyn we were going to London.

When I applied to be a reporter to the children's hearings , a degree was essential. Some had law degrees, some community social work first degrees were in the mix too. A post graduate degree set them apart and when I informed the interview panel that it was a MA in African Area studies, eyes were raised. I awaited their reaction. The chairman simply said, 'Well we asked for candidates to have a degree under their belts. Yours is a post graduate degree, somewhat unusual, but shows ability to work at such an advanced academic level. Mr Caldwell you will be reporter and a vacancy exists at Kilmarnock.'

6

In the limelight

Some professions like those of clerics, parliamentarians and news readers live in the limelight. Some find themselves thrust into that arena while others, like me, drift in and out. Of course I could have avoided each occasion but something within me felt the experience was worthwhile if not a valuable exercise.

I was aged ten years of age when my father asked me into his study. I racked my brain wondering what error or mistakes I had made to warrant such a summonsing. But instead he showed me the back of a large white envelope. I immediately recognised it was not his handwriting but his mother's, my grandmother's, who was in her twilight years.

The script took the form of a family tree. My father handed it to me to study it. He drew my attention to the bottom of the envelope to show where I fitted in and hoped I would read the line of descent from the bottom upwards. Indeed I did. My brother and sister were there, then my parents and my aunts and uncles with their children. It was a very comprehensive structure. My eyes travelled upwards to grandparents some of which I had memories and then to their parents whose names I had heard of. Then at the top of the page was a well know figure, The Bard, Robert Burns.

My father felt it was time to reveal my distinguished relative but gave a warning. He had not revealed his connection to Burns till he was at St Andrews' university. Once the word was out he received many invitations to speak about his illustrious relative and to join Burns clubs.

I took that on board for many a year. When I worked in Kilmarnock the bins declared 'For a' that an' a that, the Bins the place for a' that.' Such was the Ayrshire fondness for the Bard. But even when I was promoted to work in Ayr, nearby where the Bard was born, I stayed clear of Burns identity and their clubs.

When my final promotion to Regional Reporter to the Children's Hearings took me to Dumfries, the waters burst. I lived in digs in Dumfries before we sold-up in Troon and headed south. Retired journalist George Stevenson, (he had interviewed in his death cell Peter Manuel and worked at the UN headquarters in New York) was mine host while his wife Margaret dined and wined me almost to excess. George enquired if I had any relatives in Dumfries and Galloway and I was quick to tell him of an uncle who had been a veterinary surgeon in Thornhill. Then I made the fatal mistake, my father had warned me about. I told him the only other relative was buried here in Dumfries but that was almost 200 years ago. George's eyebrows clashed as he wondered why I had mentioned such an old relative. Then his mouth opened.

'Buried in Dumfries at St Michael's churchyard, in the Mausoleum?'

I nodded. It was Thursday night when this conversation took place and after work the following day, I returned to Troon.

On Monday, back at work in Dumfries, the telephone rang. It was Border TV. They confirmed my link to the Bard and said they would be round mid afternoon with a camera and journalist.

Sure enough I met the team who drove me to the Burns museum where I was asked to recite some poetry and be interviewed as the only living relative of the poet in the county.

Top Left to right. Relatives of Robert Burns
Jean McMillan-Foster, descendant of Robert Burn's wife Jean Armour.
Miller and his sister Mrs Joan Young; daughters Dr Laura Caldwell
and Miss Fiona Caldwell, all descendants of Robert's first child Dear
Bought Bess.

Bottom Left to Right. The top Table.
Lord Lieutenant Fiona Armstrong, Retired Director for
Education Fraser Sanderson, World Burns President Brian
Goldie, myself President DBC, Baroness Annabel Goldie House
of Lords Minister of State for Defence, The Hon David Mundell
former Secretary of State for Scotland and Provost Tracey Little.

Immediately after the word in the press and television was out in folk's homes, I received requests to join St Michael's church Burns Club, The Hole in the Wa' club, the Dumfries Burns Club and the Globe Burns Club. I was taken to the Hole in the Wa' by George but I settled in the Dumfries Burns Club established in 1820 and by far the most prestigious of Burns clubs in the country.

I served as President of the club in the year 2000 and chose as my successor Dr Ruth Thomson. She became the first female president and despite the decision causing some ruffled feathers, I was pleased to have initiated this knowledgeable Burnsian and delightful paediatrician to the position of club president.

I was asked to return to the committee many years later in 2019 and elected again for the bi-centennial year of the club's existence. On 18th December on the eve of the Covid outbreak in 2020, more than 200 people came to the Easterbrook Halls to celebrate the 200th anniversary of the Dumfries Burns Club.

Indeed the Hall was packed. They came from far and wide; from the north of Scotland, the Central belt of the country, Yorkshire, London and from Ireland too. Yet the Dumfries Burns club were few and far between. An aging club with few younger members joining had given the committee some worries. When the long standing secretary was about to hand in her resignation on age related reasons, the die was cast for me as President to end the club after 200 years in existence. That would be a drastic move for such a distinguished club. Could it possibly be saved?

I have a friend in Andrew Goss. We were both in Pakistan at the same time of the SE Asian Earthquake in 2005/6 and he made a video of my time in Pakistan, now on You Tube. He is a journalist and saw this story, rightly, as an important one.

The secretary was adamant no press release should be made and she begged me to stop the press publication. I on the other hand, failed to see why any delay was in order, and nor did I pay any heed to the Burns HQ in Kilmarnock to oversee this action I was taking. After a bitter flow of e-mails between President and Secretary, the article was published.

This had its consequences, of course. Border TV

knew it to be an important story and so I took part in a Border television News item. The result was almost a dozen new members decided to join the sinking ship. Now the challenge is to find from this enlarged membership, some committed committee members. And already Moira Weatherup has established herself as a very competent secretary, and Joe McGurk has established himself as the club's poet in residence too. Early shoots are growing. The Dumfries Burns Club has been saved.

When we arrived in Dumfries in 1992, Jocelyn had just completed a BSc in computer studies at Glasgow University and with the children grown up, wished to find work. That seemed such a daunting task, especially as, when we discussed the situation, I had to conclude prematurely. I was due at the Border TV studios in Carlisle that Friday evening to talk about child care and the Scottish system.

I recall suggesting to my wife she should prepare her CV and then approach any of the three large employers. The Police, Social Work department and the Education department, were my thoughts. That is what I felt I would do in her situation.

There were lawyers, social workers and myself being interviewed in Carlisle. The Scottish Children's Reporter Administration is known in Scandinavia, the Reporter in France is known as le Juge des Enfants but in England there was little knowledge of the post's workings. As a consequence when I informed the audience that apart from employing a reporter and securing a venue, there were no other costs involved. Panel members were volunteers and we only used the Courts if grounds were denied or an appeal of the case was to be heard. And supervision orders were undertaken by social workers.

I learned that children in England went to court. That was wrong in my opinion. Courts were never built for children and it stigmatises youngsters. The professionals were eating out of my hand and after the programme ended we continued our discussion and I felt I had made the case to enlighten the English legal system, in relation to child offenders and children who are the victims of physical, sexual and emotional abuse.

We may not know for certain why that did not launch a review of child prosecutions in England but it could not have come at a worse time.

In February 1993 James Bulger a two year old boy from Kirkby Merseyside was abducted, tortured then murdered by two 10 year olds, namely John Venables and Robert Thompson. Their names were broadcast and the public outcry was long and loud. Their cases were held in November the same year, at Preston Crown Court. It was the horrific murder of an innocent 2 year old child by two ten year olds that sealed the Hearings fate that year. The case was unique in its brutality, in the age of the victim and in the ages of the accused. The Sheriff courts in Scotland would have treated the case in a different fashion. Names would not have been divulged, cases would have been heard behind closed doors and the Sheriff court had the option of requesting the children's hearing to make a recommendation in the case. But any support for the children's hearings to be launched in England, were dealt a fatal blow because of the Bulger case.

I returned from Carlisle after midnight and woke up around 8am the following Saturday morning. Jocelyn sat up in bed with a smile on her face. Gone was the gloomy look she had, as I set off for Carlisle the night before. She just had to explain.

'I've to start work on Monday, at the Police station.'

My mouth was agape for a moment as I came to terms with her statement. Apparently, as soon as I left, Jocelyn started to write her CV and at 9 pm, as I was being interviewed on television, she walked down to the police station and enquired if they had a computer department. The reception Sergeant's eyes widened and his smile was as wide as the Solway Firth. Despite the late hour the computer manager was at his desk still working. He put a call through to Ken Carew and an impromptu interview took place that night. Of course he would have to give a formal interview and the appropriate salary but on a typist's earnings he appointed her to start work on Monday. As I type amid the Covid work-at-home provisions, I hear the tickety tack of the keyboard upstairs as a police procedure is being tackled online. I could ask her what exactly she does as a software developer with the Scottish Police, but either I'd not understand the answer or I'd be shot at dawn if I was told. It's a secret service she provides.

Early retirement before I became an author, meant afternoon tea at Countdown time. Words were a greater success for me, than the numbers, unless the total to calculate was in low two or three figures. Then Tâche would be taken for a walk and when the Border collie and I returned, I was able to see The Weakest Link before making the evening meal.

After viewing many a Weakest Link, I decided to apply for the programme. This led to a general knowledge test at a Carlisle hotel. At school I won the general knowledge prize twice so I felt confident. That was not misplaced because three weeks later I was given instructions to come to London and participate in the show.

Because of distance, I was allowed to come south the day before. So I had a meal in the hotel with my sister and her husband Ian, and my best man Andrew Barnett.

I recall a taxi taking me to the studios where I assembled with the other eight contestants. Anne Robinson never ventured into the green room unlike Richard Osman and Alexander Armstrong on Pointless but we met and made competitor friends quickly. Yet each knew we still had the power to vote someone off.

We entered the quiz area which seemed vast and there on the podium looking glum, like a beached walrus, was Anne. She ran through the rules then asked us to remember Name, Age and Home town. That may have calmed most nerves. Then the game started in earnest.

When Anne turns to you and mentions your name, there is a frisson of excitement with the experience. Yet the first round of questions was easy to answer and I began to feel confident. But that's when I'm at my weakest. On the next round, a Celebrity Get Me Out of

Here question flummoxed me. I've never seen an episode of this talent show and my hesitation stalled the game. I struggled to think of a celebrity's name and finally stated 'pass.' I answered all my other questions but had given my opponents an opportunity to evict me. I've never heard my name called out by so many people before, but before half of them had, I knew the walk of shame was coming my way. I was First out.

I said something about the Ghanaian proverb Bad Dancing does not Harm the Ground (Assa bone nkum assase) in the post quiz interview, implying there was no harm in trying the quiz. And that, so far sums up my gung-ho approach to the media at large.

There's no vanity in being elected off first and that was not my motivation. I had been lulled into the comfort of my armchair answering the questions correctly in the privacy of my home. I suppose the viewer takes pleasure in seeing each contestant leave the show. I hope they enjoyed my walk of shame.

7

SLEEP

Sleep is enjoyed by most as a daily doze from birth to death. It is characterised by levels of sleep in which dream activity unwinds in the brain. Apart from dreaming, there is not much to say about sleep except in my case there have been some seminal moments.

If I was ever the subject of Desert Island Discs, my favourite tune would be Sailing By. Ron Granger's late night tune and introductory theme to the late night Shipping Forecast is heard daily at that time. It is the final tune, apart from the national Anthem, before Radio 4 goes over to the World Service. Several times a week I hear this nightly soothing tune. That will lead you to think I am a night owl, and I admit I am.

Sleep is an important part of good health and I know that, but after the world news at 10am, my wife has gone to bed, and I have taken Georgie out for a short walk, I often write. It is quiet and I can concentrate. In fact sometimes I can write until 3am. But still no bed. Switching off the computer, after saving my work of course, I disturb our collie. She gets up to see me and then looks at the front door. I don my anorak and take her on the nearby cycle path. It is the most wonderful time to be in Dumfries. Not a soul is awake and there is no traffic. I could walk up the centre of the road for miles. But when I return home, Georgie goes straight to her basket and me to mine too. I mean my bed.

One day I was tired and thought I'd go to bed for a nap. I entered the covers and slept soundly. It must have been after my 3a.m. stints of writing. When I woke it was light. I realised Jocelyn was not in bed. She must have had work on her mind. She was up. I called out her name but there was no reply.

I felt relaxed as I shaved. The sleep had worked wonders and I went downstairs. I opened the cereal cupboard and poured milk over my Shreddies. I sat down to eat them knowing my wife had started work at Police Headquarters early that morning. I finished my cereal and toasted two slices of bread. On melted butter the morning marmalade was spread evenly over the toast. I took it to the dining table after filling the kettle and switching it on. This was my morning ritual and I guess I was on automatic pilot.

I brought the teapot through and poured it into my mug. As I ate my second slice of toast I was aware of a visitor approaching the house. Heels pattered on the surface of the cobbles and I looked up. It was my wife. She must have forgotten something. Maybe her packed lunch or her handbag had been found missing when she arrived at work, perhaps. I answered the door.

Her greeting was a surprise.

'What are you eating' she asked.

'Breakfast,' I replied nonchalantly.

'At this time, she queried with contorted eyebrows.

'Why, what time is it?'

'It's 5.35 p.m. I've been working all day.'

Then it dawned on me. When I woke from my deep sleep nap, I mistook the afternoon as daybreak.

*

When we had a break, a vacation from work in Tema Ghana, there were several options open to us. A return to the school in the Ashanti region at Bekwai where Jocelyn was a teacher; Cape Coast with its slave jails, or Busua beach where I had been many years before. However we decided to go to Timbuktu in the West African former French colony of Mali. To get there we would travel up the Volta Lake from Akosombo to Yeji. It was a crowded flat bottomed boat. We shared a cabin with an African family who slept in their colourful cloths. I had to strip as my sweating skin had drenched my body. But sleep was disturbed first by the howl of a woman who had tried to commit suicide by going overboard. Death would surely be her salvation either in the jaws of a hungry crocodile or the fact she would be, like many Ghanaians, a non swimmer. But the captain made a sharp turn and the crew managed to haul her back onboard. They tied her to a rail to prevent her attempting suicide again on the voyage.

The hum of mosquitoes was a further annoyance and I was glad when day break dawned despite my lack of sleep, as I woke bitten and hoping it was a hungry male mosquito who feasted on me and not the disease carrying female of the species.

We travelled by road to Tamale and then north to the border of Upper Volta as it was named at the time. It's now the Pointless programme favourite, Burkina Faso. We crossed at Paga where I had visited before with friends many years ago and met a friendly crocodile. It lived in a large pool of water in the centre of this small town near the Burkina Faso border. The farmer nearby had a business showing visitors his crocodile. He gathered us all in a semi-circle and he gave a sharp whistle. The still water rippled then eyes appeared. It was obviously a fully grown crocodile and it swam towards the farmer. Then one limb after the other the crocodile climbed onto the land then stopped. We were invited to lift its tail and the farmer did so to prove it was safe. But did it differentiate between black skin and white? He encourages us once again and so I went forward and lifted its tail. It did not seem to mind. Mind you my heart was racing. Then we were all told to stand back as the farmer put his hand inside a wicker basket. He pulled out a young chicken. And from the side, he bowled the frightened chicken across the crocodile's mouth. The chicken found its footing and turned sharply to run away, but the crocodile so slow on the land, snapped his jaws together after pouncing on the unfortunate chicken. And that was the show over. The farmer had entertained his visitors and made some money. The crocodile returned to the water adequately fed and waited for the next whistle and a return performance.

I have sometimes recalled this dream and been eaten by the crocodile, after the farmer had coaxed me to stroke the beast. Dreams accompany our sleep. Many chapters of my books come from my dreams and so a pad of paper sits on my bedside table.

But this time we did not stop at Paga. We proceeded across the border showing our passports to the officials who I am sure did not even look beyond the front cover. We travelled squashed in the back of a Peugeot 205 van and I dozed off despite the bumpy laterite road north. My fellow travellers slept too, partly because we were wedged like Siamese twins and did not mind the familiarity.

The van went as far as Ouagadougou, the capital of the country, but another van took us to Ouahigouya almost on the Mali border. We drank anything we could find. It was dry and very hot. It was approaching 40degrees Celsius (104Fahrenheit). We had been told transport would take us across the border and deposit us on the River Niger at Mopti where we would board a boat heading for the port of Timbuktu. But no time was given. We had to keep our eyes peeled at the spot where the transport would leave. From mid-day we waited. At a few minutes after 6pm, the van arrived. In tow were several camels. We approached the vehicle and smiles appeared. We had been expected. We entered the van and had hardly gone a couple of miles when we stopped. The engine was switched off and everyone got out of the vehicle. Then we realised it was dusk and that was prayer time for the Muslims. We stood back as they murmured their rituals hoping the prayers might be for a safe journey. The van continued on its slow way avoiding the worst of the tyre-depth potholes. A few hours later we stopped again and our travelling companions wrapped themselves in their cloths and lay down on the sand to sleep. Along with the camels who were settling in the sand. We had not prepared for such a cold night, where temperatures had gone from 40 degrees in the day to something like 12 degrees when the sun went down. A 28 degree drop in temperature is a body freezing experience. We were incredibly cold. The driver saw our concern and suggested we lie beside his camels. They would provide some warmth. And these beasts seemed to know we were cold. Their warm skins soon comforted us and so in the Sahara sands of Burkina Faso on the Mali border, we slept. Not soundly as the cold air was very uncomfortable but never before nor since have I slept with a camel.

I refer you to an earlier chapter where my bed mate, the Black American lady searching for her Nigerian routes, and I shared a bed. That perhaps should have been in this chapter. But there was another woman who shared my bed, and I don't mean my wife.

My brother-in-law had moved from Devon to Redruth in Cornwall. His mother had not seen his new home which had been a farm house. So we left Dumfries and collected my mother-in-law at Wigan. After spending a few days at that Lancashire town, we set off on the long road south to Cornwall. From the M6 to the M5 we progressed, eventually running out of motorway at Exeter. It was a slow, agricultural-vehicle peppered 'A' road to Redruth thereafter, but we got there late afternoon and Gavin's cool beer was just what I needed.

Upstairs in his farmhouse was a long corridor. Gavin

and his wife Mary slept at one end and Granny was placed at the other end next to a partitioned WC. Jocelyn and I were almost half way down the straight corridor. It was my usual semi-conscious 4 a.m. rising which alerted my wife, as I have been known to sleep walk when in this condition. I headed for the loo. I think she felt I might even fall down the stairs of this unfamiliar home, but she guided me to the bathroom and returned to bed. After washing my hands, I was still unaware exactly where I was. I left the bathroom and entered the bedroom. I usually sleep on the right side of the bed and I made for that position. I entered the bed and was almost instantly asleep when I was aware of a scream. I thought it came from outside. The shreek of a fox or an off key owl, I assumed. After all this was rural Cornwall a few miles south of Redruth. I resumed deep sleep. Jocelyn came to see what had happened as I continued unconscious in this warm bed, with my widowed mother-in-law!

This particular story has been told at 90th birthday family parties, amongst other occasions too, and has become a favourite family fable, at my expense.

8

Dumfries & Galloway
First or last in Scotland?

In the country's leading author's monthly, the Writing Magazine, an author's place of writing is often published. In garden sheds, in the attic, on the train, are some of the quirky venues. All are entertaining and thought provoking. I write in Dumfries & Galloway. Having lived here since 1992, this rural idyll where time often stands still and humans are outnumbered by black-faced sheep, there are interesting communities, vibrant villages, talkative dog walkers and a general majority quick to care for each other. It's these folk in these communities which appear in my books. And you ask where do I write? That's not so interesting. I write at my computer in the lounge, with a collie by my feet.

There are some truths and interesting facts about living in the Dumfries and Galloway local authority. It's where we settled in 1992 and has been the longest time we have been anywhere in the world. It's where I intend to leave the world in the next 20 years, if not before or miraculously if a bit longer.

Robert Burns is buried in the town in the mausoleum

at St Michael's churchyard. This fact is not as widely known as too many are drawn to his birthplace instead, in Ayrshire's Alloway village. His farm at Ellisland in our county is a tourist attraction but it's a bit off the beaten track, as is the Brow Well where Burns was ill-advised by his doctor to 'take the waters'.

JM Barrie attended Dumfries Academy. He also attended Glasgow Academy where his brother taught and I was schooled, but he is not buried in the town or as others might have thought in Poets corner in Westminster Abbey but he is found in the southern facing cemetery by the Sidlaw hills at Kirriemuir. My earliest memories were of Kirrie. One further tenuous link I had with Barrie was the fact that he stayed in Gower Street, in London for a while and that is where London University's School of Oriental and African Studies is found and where I studied.

Mr and Mrs Carlyle chose to give birth to their son, Thomas, at Ecclefechan in Annandale. Now Carlyle was a bit of a curate's egg. I'd like to remember Thomas Carlyle as a mathematics teacher in Annan. I suspect he was an interesting teacher but that would not create his status. Perhaps it was because he developed a painful stomach ailment, possibly gastric ulcers that remained throughout his life, that he gained a reputation as a crotchety, argumentative, somewhat disagreeable personality. His prose style, famously cranky and occasionally savage, helped cement an air of irascibility. His pro-slavery stance sits awkwardly with us today but his works in German and the French Revolution will stand the test of time.

Ecclefechan, a village today of 746 citizens, had two other notable figures. As little more than a hamlet, it has certainly punched its weight around. Archibald Arnott's claim to fame was that on 3rd May 1821, this army doctor received instructions that should Napoleon become insensible, no English physician but Arnott was to touch him. Napoleon died on 5th May 1821 at Longwood House, Longwood, Saint Helena, Ascension and Tristan da Cunha and Arnott attended to his final days and then his post –mortem examination. The Emperor bequeathed Arnott with six hundred Napoleons (currency at the time) and the British Government gave him an additional payment of five hundred pounds. Arnott was buried in the same graveyard as Carlyle in Ecclefechan in 1855 aged 83.

The third significant Ecclefechan was William Harkness (1837-1903) He was an astronomer who found his fame in the United States. He was buried in Jersey City USA aged 65 in 1903. Not a bad trio of notable Ecclefechan citizens.

I have my own Ecclefechan memory. It is of one of the villagers, Bill Taylor, who went to Glasgow University to study history. He became a teacher at Shawlands Secondary school in Glasgow and an elder in my father's church at Shawlands Old. He was clever and so entered the Brain of Britain. He did not win, he came second. But flushed with his relative success he entered a new quiz programme whose host was Magnus Magnusson. The quiz was Mastermind. To succeed in this quiz, you have to a) know the answer and b) say it quickly and concentrate on the next question.

Bill had not learned the technique. I give you an example.

Magnus : ' Which West African country has changed it's currency to the cedi?'

Bill: 'Well many countries are becoming independent and not surprising really. After India the African countries were sure to follow. But the cedi, yes, that belongs to The Gold Coast which is now Ghana.'

Not only did he expand his answers on each question, he spoke in that slow rural south west accent which draws out the words in each vowel and consonant.

'And Mr Taylor, you had no passes and your score is four.'

'Thank you very much indeed, Mr Magnusson.'

The first mechanically propelled, two-wheeled vehicle may have been built by Kirkpatrick MacMillan a blacksmith from Keir Hill near Thornhill, in 1839. Although this claim is sometimes disputed, he is also associated with the first recorded instance of a cycling traffic offence, when a Glasgow newspaper in 1842 reported an accident in which an anonymous "gentleman from Dumfries-shire… bestride a velocipede… of ingenious design," knocked over a little girl in Glasgow and was fined five shillings. A lesser known fact, I suggest.

Dumfries and Galloway has an unenviable record of tragedy. The Quintinshill rail disaster was a multi-train rail crash which occurred on 22 May 1915 outside the Quintinshill signal box near Gretna Green in

Dumfriesshire. It resulted in the deaths of over 200 people, and is the worst rail disaster in British history.

The Quintinshill signal box controlled two passing loops, one on each side of the double-track – the Caledonian line linking Glasgow and Carlisle. (now part of the West Coast Main Line.)

At the time of the accident, both passing loops were occupied with goods trains and a northbound local passenger train was standing on the southbound main line.

The first collision occurred when a southbound troop train travelling from Larbert to Liverpool collided with the stationary local train. A minute later the wreckage was struck by a northbound sleeping car express train travelling from London Euston to Glasgow Central. Gas from the Pintsch gas lighting system of the old wooden carriages of the troop train ignited, starting a fire which soon engulfed all five trains.

Only half the soldiers on the troop train survived. Those killed were mainly Territorial soldiers from the 1/7th (Leith) Battalion, the Royal Scots heading for Gallipoli. The precise death toll was never established with confidence as some bodies were never recovered, having been wholly consumed by the fire, and the roll list of the regiment was also destroyed in the fire. The official death toll was 227 (215 soldiers, 9 passengers and three railway employees), but the army later reduced their 215 total by one. Not counted in the 227 were four victims thought to be children, but whose remains were never claimed or identified. The soldiers were buried together in a mass grave in Edinburgh's Rosebank Cemetery, where an annual remembrance is held to this day.

An official inquiry, completed on 17 June 1915 for the Board of Trade, found the cause of the collision to be neglect of the rules by two signalmen. With the northbound loop occupied, the northbound local train had been reversed onto the southbound line to allow passage of two late-running northbound sleepers. Its presence was then overlooked, and the southbound troop train was cleared for passage. As a result, both were charged with manslaughter in England, and then convicted of culpable homicide after trial in Scotland; (the two terms are broadly equivalent.) After they were released from a Scottish jail in 1916, they were re-employed by the railway company, although not as signalmen.

Princess Victoria was launched on 27 August 1946 and completed in 1947 by William Denny and Brothers, Dumbarton for the London, Midland and Scottish Railway (LMS). She was the first purpose-built ferry of her kind to operate in British coastal waters and the fourth ship to bear the name, her 1939 predecessor having been sunk during World War II in the Humber Estuary by a German mine. Although innovative in her loading methods, the vessel looked externally similar to her predecessor. She could hold 1,500 passengers plus cargo and had sleeping accommodation for 54.

The sinking of Princess Victoria occurred during a severe European windstorm which also caused the North Sea Flood of 1953, claiming 531 fatalities in the

UK alone, although this was the worst single incident in that storm. There were 135 deaths, including the Deputy Prime Minister of Northern Ireland, Maynard Sinclair and the MP for North Down, Sir Walter Smiles. There were no women or children among the survivors. Eyewitnesses reported seeing a lifeboat containing at least some of the women and children being smashed against the side of Princess Victoria by the huge waves. The disaster shocked many people because, although it took place in extreme weather conditions, it involved a routine journey, on a relatively short crossing (20 miles, 32 km) in what were believed to be safe waters.

In both Larne and Stranraer, small towns that largely relied on their seaports, most families were affected in some way. A ceremony was held in Larne; wreaths were thrown on the water and the crowd sang "Lord, hear us when we cry to thee, for those in peril on the sea".

The bodies of 100 people who died in the disaster were eventually recovered, although some of them came ashore as far away as the Isle of Man.

Dumfries and Galloway also has an unenviable record of road deaths on the M74 and other feeder roads as well. In fact they are disproportionately affected in a rural area where traffic heads north and south of the border.

We cannot and must not forget Lockerbie when Pan Am 103 crashed over the town on 21st December 1988. The American town of Syracuse in New York state and Lockerbie, Scotland are closely associated since this disaster when 270 people from 21 nations were tragically killed including 11 residents of Lockerbie, 3 of whom were school children, and 35 Syracuse University students. Annual scholarships called "Lockerbie Scholars" and "Remembrance Scholars" were established by Syracuse University in memory of those who died. Two Lockerbie Academy pupils are welcomed and study at Syracuse University each year as "Lockerbie Scholars". My new Dumfries Burns Club secretary is a Lockerbie Scholar who studied at Syracuse University in 1992/93 through this living memorial. She attended her first Burns Night Supper in Syracuse, New York, such is the reach of the welcoming overseas Scottish community and Burns connection. An alumni of the University of Glasgow and post-graduate of the University of Stirling and Leeds Beckett University, Moira Weatherup will make a super Burns Club secretary.

Snow fell on 7th February 1996. Five died in the blizzards. For 12 days there was no traffic in Dumfries and the height of the snow at our front door was four and a half feet. Dumfries & Galloway was the worst hit not only in that year but for decades before. The only ones who could not care less were the pupils whose schools were closed for two weeks.

On February 20 2001, foot and mouth was discovered in an abattoir in Essex. Several weeks later it had travelled north and despite a ban on livestock movement, Scotland's first cases were announced here in Dumfries and Galloway on March 1, with two farms affected at Lockerbie and Canonbie. Commenting at the time,

Scottish NFU president Jim Walker said confirmation that the disease had reached Scotland was 'a tragedy for the whole industry'.

This region went on to bear the brunt of the outbreak, as many will remember. It lasted until May 23 the following year and in that time 177 premises were affected locally.

According to Scottish Executive records, 544,309 animals were slaughtered in total across Dumfries and Galloway and burning pyres became a common sight, and horrendous odour with the army brought in to help with the gruesome task. Some of the animals were killed as part of contiguous culls, following the introduction on March 15 of a 3km firebreak around infected farms to try and stop the disease in its tracks.

However, it later emerged that many of the flocks slaughtered on suspicion were later reported to have been – test negative. And there were several court cases as desperate small holders tried to save their pets – some successful, others not. Over £1 billion was paid out in compensation to affected farmers nationwide.

But they were not the only ones affected, with a big hit on the rural economy and tourism decimated too, as the countryside was effectively closed off.Meanwhile, after a string of visits to the region by leading politicians, including the First Minister Henry McLeish and Prime Minister Tony Blair, the General Election was postponed by a month due to the Foot and Mouth events.

And on 19th November 2021 the NHS put out a warning:

'Members of the public are being advised to avoid interacting with wild birds in the region, and to report any discoveries of sick or dead birds.'

An assessment of a 'very low' risk to public health is being offered, following the confirmation of at least one case of H5N1 avian flu within Dumfries and Galloway. Consultant in Public Health Medicine Dr Nigel Calvert said: 'Our region is well known as a popular location for migratory birds at this time of year. Other countries and other areas of Scotland have recently seen reports of visiting birds falling ill with the H5N1 avian flu, so it was not unexpected that we would also see cases within Dumfries and Galloway – given the numbers that visit each year.

"In recent days a number of birds have fallen ill along the Solway Coast. Tests are taking place, following confirmation of an initial case of H5N1 in a swan. The risk to the public from this strain of avian flu is very low. However, it is important that people do not touch any sick or dead birds. We would ask anyone who identifies a sick or dead bird to please contact the Department for Environment, Food and Rural Affairs (Defra) in the first instance by phoning 03459 335577. If anyone has recently handled a sick or dead bird, especially without benefit of personal protective equipment, they can receive advice by contacting Public Health on 01387 246246.

Finally, as a precautionary measure, warning signs are being erected at some locations along the Solway Coast to advise of the current situation in respect of migratory birds, while testing continues to take place."

At Stranraer, Lockerbie and at Edinburgh for Quentinhill's dead, memorial services are conducted annually. We honour the dead.

Quite a succession of hits for D&G, I suggest. Just imagine that Quintinshill signal man thinking, this is the worst rail crash ever. Thank God, there will be no more disasters. He might have thought or said that and the people of Stranraer on seeing the MV Princess Victoria go down, that that must be the worst peacetime drowning, oh never again should we have a disaster in D&G. And after the multiple deaths on the motorways, the Lockerbie air disaster, Foot and Mouth and Avian Flu, who is not to think the first meteor to hit the UK will perhaps descend in Dumfries & Galloway? After all we have experience of calamity. A sobering thought.

9

S to the power of 4
SCRA SOAS SOAiS SASO

People populate my books. I meet them in many spheres of life. No more so than in the associations I have and continue to enjoyed.

First of course is my twenty year career as a reporter to the **SCRA** Scottish Children's Reporter Administration. I can now see the system from an arm's length and it is not always rosy. Hearings place children on supervision requirements. It is the over worked child care social workers who have to fulfil the contract between the hearing decision and their work with children.

When local authorities continue to shave off the funding for departments, it results in fewer social workers in the child care field. That leads to pressures on the supervision of children and, if neglected, we see such cases earn the media's wrath. Will SCRA survive? Yes, it will because of its cost effectiveness. Find a suitable place to hold the hearings, employ a reporter and that's all. Panel members are voluntary and apart from travel remuneration, that's the total expenditure. You can't get a juvenile offending and abused children system cheaper than that.

My Scottish colleagues are no more than 108 in the country and at one time I knew them all. Some wore their kilts to work but all were in dark suits when in court prosecuting the denied grounds or defending the hearing's decisions in appeals. Over the years the preponderance of male reporters have been overtaken by females and that's no bad thing. I began in Kilmarnock with four male reporters and ended my career in Dumfries when I was the token male reporter in a team with five female reporters.

I am the Scottish representative of the School of Oriental and African Studies, London University. **SOAS.** There aren't any SOAS graduates in D&G at present and not many in Scotland. I called a meeting of Scottish graduates and found all could attend in Edinburgh. They numbered 12. Many graduate from London University's School of Oriental and African Studies and join the ranks of the Foreign Office. They can be found in positions of seniority in Ambassadorial circles around the world. All twelve I met, had gone on to work as teachers or in business concerns with interests in Africa or Asia.

For professions seeking graduates without specific degree qualifications, the university's standing may be the deciding factor in selecting the candidate. London's SOAS consistently is in the UK top ten of universities. Perhaps that must have been a factor in my appointment as a reporter.

SoAiS. The Society of Authors in Scotland is the northern branch of its parent body, The Society of Authors. It is the writer's trade union advising of tax affairs and contracts, advising about agents and arbitrating when appropriate, on behalf of its members. I was appointed to serve on its committee and became the events manager. I also attended the Society's AGM at their London offices. (Making it an opportunity for me to meet up with my sister and her husband and my best man too.)

I set up a local book day at the library in Locharbriggs, where three authors and three poets spoke. But setting up other book festivals in the country from Dumfries meant the computer and zoom facilities were used to the full.

I also zoom on the UK Society of Authors with disability or chronic illnesses. We are the underrepresented authors with a variety of life restricting ailments and disabilities. Some are well hidden like mental illnesses while others are very visible as wheelchair authors. I'm in between with mild cognitive impairment, rheumatoid arthritis in my left knee and now Parkinson's disease.

SASO. The Scottish Association for the Study of Offending. I joined when it was known as SASD in Stirling in 1984. There was no branch in Ayrshire when we moved there neither in Ayr nor Kilmarnock but I resumed membership in Dumfries where I have been its chair for over twelve years. SASD began shortly after Lord Kilbrandon initiated SCRA through his 1964 report. The association began referring to delinquency in its title. However that was changed to Offending; an all inclusive word covering the offending child and offending adult against a child or children. 'Offending' was chosen to replace Delinquency and so by the time

I joined the Dumfries branch, it was The Scottish Association for the Study of Offending.

Being the authority closest to Ireland and England, my creative mind felt it would be good to see how each of the three nations, all except Wales, treated its child offenders and child victims. I travelled to Carlisle and to Belfast to speak to their police forces and gained interest in this conference. When I arrived in Belfast we had a very useful logistics meeting in the morning and then we set out in an unmarked car and entered a travel shop. I was instructed to follow close behind. When we entered, the Inspector greeted the lady behind the desk and we went through a door behind her. Through a corridor we walked to an increasing volume of conversation and when the next door opened, we were in a restaurant, where the occupants of tables stood up to acknowledge the chief inspector's presence but all eyes were on me, who followed on.

Such were the necessary precautions the RUC took in those troubled years to entertain their guests. At the end of the day, I was driven to the port and handed a brown envelope with the instruction not to open it till I was back in Scotland. I gave my word.

However, I was on the last sailing of the night and the ship was not over populated. I made for a quiet corner of the lounge and took out the package. I opened it and felt it. It seemed to contain a few small stones. I opened my cupped hand and tipped the envelope up. Out slid not one but three buttonhole badges. The Red hand of Ulster was one badge, another was the six counties of Northern Ireland in relief and the last, a RUC Royal Ulster Constabulary button badge. I smiled to myself.

What a red face I'd have, if not a gun to my head, if I had opened it before I embarked aboard the ship and it was seen by the wrong person.

Six weeks later, Irish and Cumbrian voices mingled with ours in the Municipal halls where we held the SASO conference and a discussion took place as we each gave our evidence of how we treated youth offenders and the offended against. In attendance were SASO members from the central belt, seeing this as an important conference. So too were the press in attendance.

To Canada we also went to study prisons in Ottawa and at Kingston, Canada's former and exposed capital city. We went there in early March 1998. It was not only cold, it was very snowy. One free day was the first Sunday and I carefully walked along the Rideau Canal from the hotel towards the Ottawa River. I had last seen the spectacular river in summer 1971. After working at Camp Onota in Massachusetts, I went to Canada to meet long lost relatives in Ottawa and then Winnipeg in Manitoba. But in 1971 the river was a floating expanse of logs. I learned the logs were heading to match factories where smokers would soon have their match boxes, for their pipes and cigarettes, in their pockets. In those days passengers smoked on flights, people smoked in cafes, on busses and trains; in fact almost anywhere. Twenty seven years later not one log was to be seen. It may have been mid-winter but instead of logs there were a few growlers* in the river. And I don't mean polar bears.

* A "growler" is a colloquial term and collective noun applied to icebergs of small mass, which therefore only show a small portion above the surface.

I was struck by the number of native Indians who were detained in secure accommodation. (I believe the term is now First Nation Americans.) Many were murderers but the most humble of men in their custodial, alcohol-free entrapment made them seem harmless. Maybe they had been tranquilised into submission. I cannot tell but they were interested in our interest, in them.

We were a party of ten representatives of SASO and each of us had to prepare a report on a custodial visit. I gave a report on the Ottawa William Hay Centre. I now quote from Journal 4 of the paper an interesting fact:

"Like many cities, Ottawa is divided by a river. However the Ottawa, frozen over during our visit, separates more than a town. On the conservative Ontario bank it is illegal to buy cigarettes until the age of 19 years. On the liberal Quebec bank the corresponding age is 13 years. The Alexandra bridge supports Ottawa's pedestrian teenagers as their differing culture, politics and laws clash." MC

The Scottish Journal of Criminal Justice Studies –
Volume 4 August 1998.

10

Was I A Russian Spy?

Holidays in my youth were often at Fairlie where my grandmother lived, on the Ayrshire coast. Her home in Southannan Drive was a bungalow with a long garden in which we played French Cricket. Those were warm summers in those days and made such a contrast to inward rural Kirriemuir and later urban Newlands in Glasgow. Fairlie lost its appeal when the Hunterston Nuclear Power Station B was erected on the village shoreline. The water around the bay became warmer. That was a signal to bathe elsewhere and in 1967 we did.

Not many people holiday on Jura. Those who might find themselves on that lonely island would certainly not stay much beyond a few days, having climbed the Paps of Jura perhaps. Today there is an exclusive golf course. Private to all intents and purposes, it welcomes those who know their golf, enjoy a challenge and can afford a day's play. The 'full day golf experience' costs **£1,300 plus VAT** while a room in The Quads, the centrepiece of the on-site accommodation apart from Jura House itself, starts at £900 per night. I can appreciate this is one of the world's best courses and is not one for the rookie but I can't see many of us heading there no matter what our golf handicap might be. That is unless you won the Lottery.

The course designer, Bob Harrison (Robert William Harrison born NSW Australia in 1949) must have been an eighteen year old engineering student, when we visited there in the sixties. Jura had one road leading to the distillery, the only employment on the island in this sparsely populated Hebridean idyll. Maybe if you had a boat, you could visit or assess the treacherous cauldron of the Corryvreckan whirlpool from the safety of land. Or if you possessed a literary gene, visit the cottage at Barnhill if you need to imbibe the presence of George Orwell (aka Eric Blair) who completed *Nineteen Eighty-Four* at Barnhill on the north of the island. That's about all you can do on Jura, which is why not many go there. That however may be its attraction.

We were there, not for a few days or even a week, let alone a fortnight. Dad had packed four sermons and our month on Jura had begun. There were of course some stunning beaches for warm dry picnics but westerly winds were common that summer and cardigans were in evidence. I had brought a couple of books but had read them. A few comics too and they were read from cover to cover with their crosswords completed. I was bored and moody and this holiday niggled me. My older sister and younger brother must have wished I had not come on holiday with them, as my attitude was plain to see. It was therefore no surprise that my mother let me take the family radio with me to listen to it on the hill behind our holiday home.

I began to climb up the steep hill. I saw my very first adder sunning itself on a warm bolder. I gave it a wide berth and carefully avoided placing my footing on heather where its relatives might be. However I found an even larger bolder in the sun and sat down to enjoy its warmth. I placed the radio on my knee and switched it on. The Light service was not interesting and the Home service just as dull. I turned the dial to short wave and fiddled with the positioning. A programme in French emerged and I lay back to discover how much I could understand. But the actors spoke very quickly and I did not even get a gist of the production. I sat up and continued to spin the wheel of the Bush radio dial. It then alighted on a farming programme. I gave up. I lay back to sunbathe but the wireless stayed on.

I could have fallen asleep but began to take an unusual interest in the programme. I heard it speak of Ayrshire cows, a common breed in England! Then a few minutes later, the black faced sheep on the high ground of Norfolk.

I sat up wondering if it was a comedy but no further clues to the mistakes surfaced, until the programme ended. I had been listening to Radio Moscow's faming programme to the UK. Why was the programme so poorly researched was my first thought? I sat for a moment with the radio turned off. The mistakes just did not leave my mind. Then I had a plan. I returned home.

In my bedroom that night when all were in bed, I took out a fresh white sheet of paper and wrote about the mistakes and why they were wrong. I addressed the letter to Radio Moscow, Moscow, Russia, and then fell asleep. The following morning I walked the quarter of a mile to the lonely letter box on the island which rarely felt a letter drop inside most days. It may not even reach its destination, I wondered. I had plastered a few stamps on it without verifying the true postage cost. How could I? The post office was not on the island. I had completed my errand and thought nothing more about it.

That was until a week after we returned home, after that uneventful holiday when evening scrabble was the highlight of most evenings. I received a letter.

It was from London, the office of the Russian Ambassador to the UK. The missive was an apology for the mistakes in the programme as well as a programme of listings for Radio Moscow in the UK. In addition was a photo of a Russian girl, Kristina Kuznetsova, probably two years older than myself. She was a student of the prestigious Moscow State University where she was in her second year of chemical engineering. Her photo was stunning. She was blond and her hair almost covered one eye. I could not help feel it was a provocative pose. And it was appealing to my eye. I kept her photo in my wallet and showed my friends at school to their total envy.

I wrote a few times to Kristina and she asked me to correct her English but her English was actually quite good for a science student, I thought.

My school days were coming to an end and I too would be a student in Edinburgh, and I told my exciting news to Kristina.

Not long afterwards I received a letter from the Russian Ambassador's office. I opened it wondering what the Ambassador might say, but then a cheque flew out and landed on the table. It was a sterling cheque of £800.00 to see me through my first year of university.

I had never seen such a large amount with my name being the one to whom it was paid. £800 in 1969 was a lot of money. I had found digs in Joppa for £5 a week for example. With a father on a less remunerative salary as a church minister I had also acquired the maximum student grant. I was flush with money but with a growing dilemma. '…see me through my first year?' What about the second, third and fourth years? There was an implication that this was to be an annual payment. Then I would receive further instalments. My reporting faults in their broadcasting seemed to be over compensated but I thought no more about that. Serendipity. I had never experienced such a wealthy feeling.

And I leave you with that thought, for the rest of the story and my time as a Russian Spy is contained in the book 'Caught in a Cold War Trap.' This book was taken on board by Los Angles film script writer Dan Guardino, who has given me the film script, so you may want to see the film in due course. If you wish to see the film script, please e-mail me at:

netherholm6@yahoo.com

11

My time in Prison

I had been in many prisons in Canada through SASO, you will recall. My friend David Benrexi, the singer song writer of Camp Onota days, from South Carolina; visited us in Dumfries. We toured prisons in Scotland and in the north of England singing his songs and entertaining the captured audiences. (Listen to David Benrexi on You Tube).

However I received a telephone call one day from the governor of Dumfries prison. Chrissie McGeever knew I was an author and wondered if I could solve one of her problems. Dumfries prison had detainees for pre sentencing and pre trial, sex offenders and the run of the mill offenders. All these groups had to be kept apart for security reasons. However, the prison also had a wing in which 12 girls, or should I say young women, were detained. The issue was that the women were deprived movement around the building to the dining room and the recreation yards, as this would involve meeting male prisoners. I was invited to be the writer in residence with the specific remit to educate and engage with the women, in recompense for their solitude.

On my first day, I was surprised to discover that I

knew four of the women. I had known them as girls, in fact children who had appeared before me as the reporter and I remember their supervision requirements with conditions such as to attend school regularly, to have access or denial to an absent parent; or to have their supervision requirement reviewed in four months and not await the annual review. I could have been detested. However I was welcomed by open arms as someone who was not a prison officer and so was someone they could make demands to. They demanded sweets. I brought some and they all took a fudge square but knew to stop chewing as soon as an officer appeared. If caught eating their gullible writer in residence and fall guy would be a lost to them. True, I felt sorry for them. Poor parental care and mixing with the wrong crowd had marred their schooldays and now the majority of them had graduated to make some money transporting drugs.

One West African woman was bullied and kept herself to herself. She was Nigerian and was about to be deported as an illegal immigrant. She was depressed, unrepresented legally and unsure what would happen next. She had arrived in Eire and from there she travelled to Northern Ireland but she was detained when she arrived at Stranraer when she got off the ferry. I asked to see her, by virtue of my West African knowledge. I was taken to her cell. I told her about some of my experiences working in Ghana and she was genuinely interested to meet me. It transpired she could not understand the English spoken by the local women and so she had not engaged with them. Some words were understood but had derogatory overtones for her and so her depression continued. I promised I would speak for her but felt she needed to be part of the female prisoners until her case was settled. I came out with her to join the group. I asked the local female prisoners how they would feel if they found their selves in a Nigerian prison with no white prisoners to talk to. There was a hush. I informed them they should treat her with the respect they themselves enjoyed. I told them that Mercy was her name and she lived in a small rural village and her first language was Yoruba. Crocodiles were there in the ponds by the village and so I told them I had written about a crocodile in a poem. My prisoners now had an agenda to find how living in Africa was and the reservations subsided.

The very next day, I gave them a poem which I recently wrote. Mercy was very much part of the group now. They enjoyed the story. Some of the more arty women drew pictures to accompany the text and the book took

Daughter Fiona with a Sierra Leone crocodile.

shape. Chaz the Friendly Crocodile is a children's first book. At the end, the child is asked to sign a contract not to carry knives or drop litter etc. The class teacher signs the contract too as well as the parent(s). This is the poem I wrote in half an hour. You can imagine me walking our collie Tâche by the river Nith to the rhythm of the poem.

The poem and song.

A Crocodile born in Nigeria was sad and lonely all day
Born with no teeth to eat or kill or hunt its prey.
It saw no future in Africa, life was really so sad
No friend came to play on the Niger River
Yet he was so good and not bad.

A migrating swallow then spoke to it.
It came from the old river Nith.
It told of friendly people,
'Doonhamers' their kin and their kith.

So the Crocodile swam and it swam,
It swam and swam every day.
The water grew colder and colder
Then it reached the shores of Solway.

From there to Dumfries was a doddle,
He found home on a bank near Lochside
And a friend, aged five, called Peter
Met him each day at low tide.

To make himself really useful,
Peter asked if he'd do a few jobs.
Like clean the river of rubbish,
Of prams and mobiles and knobs.

The Police were exceedingly happy.
Lost property lay on the banks.
Most were returned to their owners
Who reclaimed them with grateful thanks.

The town's regular winter flooding
Got the Council greatly involved.
But dredging was in the Croc's nature
So the flooding was permanently solved.

Early every morning,
Between the hours of two and of three
The Croc would leave the river
And the town he'd go to see

His sharp claws scrapped the streets,
The chewing gum did vanish
And with his tail, he wiped away
Graffiti words to banish.

At lambing time each year,
Farmers counted all their flocks
Exposure to frost claimed some,
For others the hungry hawks.

Some fell into the Nith,
Wandering through a broken gate
But the Crocodile scooped up many
Which saved the lambs from their fate.

Then quite by chance the Croc discovered,
His teeth were at last growing
This put at risk the boys and girls
Who used the Nith for rowing.

So Peter said that home
Is where he now should spend his days
But thanks to him, the Crocodile,
We've learned to mend our ways.

The Croc has returned to the Niger
And he's happy to greet every friend.
He tells of his days in cold Scotland
And the things he was able to mend.

But this tale is more than a story,
It's a lesson to learn this day.
Keep your town and river tidy,
It's great if it looks that way.

FOR
IF YOU DO NOT REMEMBER
THEN GUESS WHAT YOU WILL FIND?
A CROCODILE WITH SHARP TEETH
MIGHT HAVE YOUR NAME IN MIND

This is your Promise and your Contract

To keep your Town, City or Village tidy and clean
To behave properly and you'll be proud to be seen.

Now sign Your Contract with the help of your parent and teacher.

I .... (Name)

Of .... (Address)
....

I promise to keep my playground, the streets and busses of our town .... clean.

I will not drop litter or chewing gum. Instead I will place litter in a bin or bring my litter home.
I will not write on walls or park seats.
I will not swear even when someone swears at me.
I will not smoke or take illegal drugs which kill many each year.
I will never bully anyone but report bulling to my teacher, my parents or a police officer.
I promise never to carry a knife or a gun.
I understand that many children will join me in making this promise and as a result we will have clean towns and happier people in our country.

Signed by you, the pupil

....

Signed by your parent

....

Signed by your Class teacher

....

Signed by Chaz the Crocodile

....................**Chaz**................

My time at Dumfries Prison came to an end. There were no women left. No, I did not forget to lock the doors but so few women were eventually incarcerated that it was decided that the remaining women would go to Greenock Prison or the exclusively female prison at Cornton Vale in the Central belt. That did little to promote necessary family links.

Chaz the Friendly Crocodile is in many children's homes and some of the primary schools. The police have also used the book to instil good behaviour in our young citizens. Had I not been the writer in residence in Dumfries prison, I'd not have befriended Mercy, perhaps this story may not have been published. But that's how a book came out of this.

I have returned to prison twice. I was a prison visitor.

Men who were far from home welcomed such outside contact. One man was quite distinguished. He had held the award of OBE for his service to the community. But he served it too well and women began to provide evidence of his sexual abuse at his hands. Contrite he was but he knew when he was eventually released he would be on the sex offenders register and his honour withdrawn.

My last incarcerated visits were not actually in prison but police cells where the alleged offender was located prior to a first court appearance. They too welcomed the outside visitors. One had to be careful what one said nevertheless as they might fly off the handle if challenged.

One farmer was in his cell. I entered. Did he have a wife?' I asked presuming that would be a welcomed gesture. 'Would she be visiting?'

'No, he said, 'I nearly killed her. That's why I'm in here.'

Shortly afterwards, I collapsed when gathering brambles. My wife found me on the grass, fortunately it was a Sunday afternoon and she was at home. I had suffered a seizure. After tests, I was not allowed to drive for a year, so my police cell visitation came to an abrupt end, and the start of a regime of pills became a necessary medication from then on.

12

A Square Peg in a Round Hole

I sometimes see life differently from others. It is as if I don't quite fit in with expectations. I give the following examples.

I had received a shopping list at work in Kilmarnock. With two young children and a frequently house-bound wife, it was not a chore to end work and go to the supermarket to make these purchases. One day I had completed my shopping chore and entered the queue at the till. Then it was my turn and as I prepared to empty my shopping bags, I saw another cashier approach and fill the till with a packet of £1 coins. She bent over and I noticed both had the same name tags. 'Ah sisters,' I declared. They focussed all four eyes in my direction. I clarified my thoughts. 'Two Polish names, the same, Chekouts, so I thought you must be …well…sisters.' The staff looked at their name tags and indeed they were the same.

One thrust her badge towards me. 'See here,' she said tapping a finger on her badge. 'C H E C K O U T S,' she responded. We're nay sisters.' And on reflection, they had nothing in common.

*

On another occasion, I was asked to cover a children's hearing for an ill colleague at Dalry, in north Aryshire. I had never been to the Walker Hall in this town before, so I set of earlier than was necessary to ensure I found the venue. Indeed the town not being too large, I found it in the centre. I parked behind the community building and met the caretaker who ensured there would be no activity in the hall so that the hearing would be in privacy. I thanked him and made my way to the room. A long table had been laid out and the panel members arrived. I introduced myself and the first case was called. I am not allowed to mention the name of the offending child by name. But like my first name or Murray or Martin, this child had a Scottish surname as a forename. The hearing took just under the hour and I took from my file a sheet of paper to place the child under the care of the social work department for a period of a year, after which time the case would appear for an annual review. I filled out the details of the child and then passed the supervision requirement to the chairman who duly signed. I looked at him in anticipation to have the requirement returned to me, but I was perplexed by his next comment.

'I can't sign this,' he said.

I looked confused. The date was on the sheet as well as the venue Dalry and the boy's name. What could he mean?

The chairman returned the sheet to me. 'You've placed the hall on supervision,' he said. Sure enough Walker Hall was now subject to a supervision requirement.

However it was soon adjusted to the correct name and the family never knew the mistake I had made, nor did they hear the panel members' laughter.

*

Promotion is normally a pleasing event. It meant a new patch in south Ayrshire having started in North Ayrshire. The trouble began a few weeks before, after a social cup of tea following a panel training session in the evening in Kilmarnock. The subject on that cold winter's night was hot-water bottles. In a standing position a group of six or so panel members and myself, heard that some had stone water bed warmers, some had electric blankets while others had both rubber bottles and hand knitted hot water bottles. It was not perhaps the most erudite of discussions but it had not ended until the reporter was asked what was in his bed. I informed them that I never needed a hot water bottle because I was naturally hot in bed. Some laughed. Others asked what the joke was and then laughed. The joke was on me, the man who was hot in bed.

A few weeks later this story was recalled as I attended a farewell meeting in Irvine's Rivergate House. Then I was off to Ayr. A new set of panel members and new hearing venues in Ayr, Cumnock, Troon, Girvan and Dalmellington. I was initiated at a panel members' training night as the new Area reporter and introduced by the chair as the man who was hot in bed. How that story crossed over from north to south Ayrshire, I'll never know but it put a smile on the female panel members' faces in Ayr. I'm glad to say that the story did not cross into D&G where my final promotion took me.

*

One of my most infuriating regular encounters is with bank officials. I may have transferred some money or paid a BACS bill but when the service is completed, they often ask; 'Is there anything else I can do for you'. As it happens I tend to get the bank business over before I complete the shopping chore so I give the surprised bank official my shopping list. Of course the list is returned with a smile. Not at the prank played but in seeing the error of his ways. Somehow it has caught on with other office staff and they all get the same treatment.

*

My next pitfall was my second visit to Crosshouse hospital in Kilmarnock. I was to have my turbinates cauterised. The bone in the nose reduced, for those unfamiliar with the procedure. I expected everything to go as smoothly as my first nasal operation the previous year. How wrong I was!

I made my way to Ward 3B and given a bed. The ward nurse remembered me and remarked that I would not have forgotten the ropes. I agreed. I confidently secured the irreversible studded nameplate round my left wrist only to see it drop onto the polished floor seconds later. A new band was brought and fastened in the style of a double clove hitch by a dismayed nurse.

I was sitting up in bed now with a thermometer under my left arm at the same time as presenting my right arm to have my blood pressure checked. It was normal but where was the thermometer? In concentrating on the pressure being applied to my right arm, I had let slip the pencil thin thermometer from my left armpit. It lay beneath my pyjamas in two pieces. I reflected on another unnecessary expense to the NHS.

The shower room with its adjacent loo was already lit on my entry to provide a urine sample. I obliged with a modest sample, tugged the suspended light switch cord frantically noticing the plastic red button at the end, too late.

'Don't worry Mr. Caldwell, you are not the first to pull the emergency help button', reassured the quietly exasperated nurse. I felt I deserved a £50 fine!

I settled into the ward and made acquaintance with my fellow patients. We each revealed our medical problems that had brought us together and shared our anticipated length of stay in confinement with each other. I explained that I was a prosecutor of juveniles in court – a reporter to the children's panels.

That information led to sharing the story of the Sheriff some time ago who lived in Troon and relied on friends to run him to work at the Kilmarnock Sheriff Court some nine miles away. One morning he accepted a lift from a lorry driver. As they reached the 40mph limit on the outskirts of town the lorry slowed down to 32mph. On reaching the 30mph limit, the driver slowed down to 22mph.

'Taking it easy?' enquired the Sheriff.

'Aye, there's a bastard of a Sheriff in Kilmarnock an' I'm no losing my licence over him,' the driver said, staring straight ahead.

On reaching the centre of town the Sheriff, still travelling incognito, asked to be dropped off. As the lorry pulled into the kerb, the grateful passenger took a £10 note from his wallet and thrust it into the lorry driver's hand.

'There. That's from your friendly bastard, the Sheriff!'

As the recently acquired captive audience showed their appreciation of the story, an elderly man stirred from the bed to my left.

'It was only £5, sir, and I should know. I was the Sheriff.'

The anaesthetic could not come quickly enough.

*

Ride the Dignes to Nice train calling at 18 stations, picking up school children on its way. That's how to immerse oneself in the French way of life. Relaxing while looking at the French countryside en Provence on a warm June afternoon on the most picturesque rail route between Dignes and Nice, a young boy with a bottle of half drunk water came through to our carriage.

"Monsieur, avez vous de Scotch?"

Well, I just shook my head and thought what is the next generation coming to? Here in rural France a school boy was obviously mixing his last drop of water with any passenger's hip flask of whisky. What a brass neck!

But to my surprise an elderly Madame rummaged in her shopping bag and produced some Scotch! She handed it to the delighted school boy who sat down and used the Scotch tape to repair his torn exercise book! Je m'excuse mes amis. En Ecosse nous avons Le Whisky et Le Sellotape! Mais pas de Scotch!

*

Had I not been abused and sought refuge in West Africa, my life could have been very much different. I could have been an actor.

I acted as Hopcroft minor in the 1950 comedy – farce: The Best Days of Your Life, by John Dighton. I improvised by having one stocking down at my ankles and a black eye as the school boy in the play. We had a lively amateur dramatic ensemble at the church and after this performance I played the drums at the annual Christmas pantomime. These roles gave me the confidence, the desire and the guts to continue on stage at school as each year as I appeared in the Gentleman's chorus, in various settings. But in my final year I was Dick Whittington. That was the lead role in the pantomime of the same name. That spring I applied to go to RADA, on the crest of a wave but my acting was not on a par with other would-be actors and I was asked to get more experience and re-apply in a year's time. By then I was at college studying social work.

*

It was not really my mistake this time. Gran died in November 2021 aged 98. A good innings for such a dedicated cricket fan and we were comforted by recalling her long life. A Bletchley Park encrypter, a doctor's wife and mother of two children, a keen gardener, ornithologist and bridge player. Much to remember. However, following a stroke, for the past few years she had been resident in a care home in Wigan, Lancashire. We visited her one sunny day and found her sitting up in bed. Her smile greeted us.

'So Gran anything to report?'

'Umm, let me see. Oh yes. Rose is dead.'

'Very sorry to hear that. Everything else ok?' I asked not finding a death as unsurprising in a care home for the very elderly.

'Yes for the time being.'

I whispered to my wife, noticing Gran's hearing aid by her bedside.

'Joce did you know Rose died?'

'Rose? I don't know of anyone she knows called Rose.'

We put our heads together but could not figure it out who Gran meant.

'Mum, let me clarify. You said Rose is dead?' said Jocelyn a little perturbed. Is that correct?'

'Yes dear. Roses dead. Remember the roses you gave me in June? Well sorry to say they are dead but I enjoyed them in bloom when they lasted.'

*

I had donated blood on more than ten occasions. It meant I could sport a blood donor's pin badge but the next time I appeared, after going through the list of questions the nurse always had, she mentioned the word Malaria. I don't recall them asking that before.

'One moment please,' she said and set off to the room in which the doctor sat. She returned a moment later.

'I'm sorry, sir, we cannot take your blood.'

'Why was it blue I jested?'

But she kept her solemn face. 'You say you have had Malaria.'

'Yes twice. But it's West African malaria not East African,' I said in my defence.

She looked confused. 'Malaria is malaria, sir.'

'Yes, but West African malaria does not reoccur in inclement weather here. Rev J Watt at New College in Edinburgh always wore spats because he had had the Eat Africa malaria. But West African malaria, which incidentally I last had more than twenty years ago, is not contagious, it does not reoccur in Europe.'

Armed with my information she returned to consult the doctor. This time she took longer to return. I felt sure a reference book was being consulted and would prove me right.

'She returned without a smile. 'I'm afraid we can't accept your blood donation. There is a minimal risk that you could pass it to a patient and we would be responsible. We cannot take that risk.' Then she smiled a little. 'You can still have a cup of tea and a biscuit though.'

*

That reminded me of a story:

In the UK we donate blood to the hospitals free. In return there is refreshment.

It was John's first date. He took out his new girlfriend Joan. On her return home, Joan's mother asked her if the date went well.

"Oh, yes mum. It was very exciting. We had tea and biscuits".

'Really? Was that all there was to the date?' asked Mum.

'Yes, but I had never given blood before.'

*

Orkney and the Western Isles have been our holiday destinations recently, to visit relatives on Orkney and enjoy walks on Harris and Lewis. In fact the Western Isles have influenced my niece's name, Iona, and our daughter's dog is called Harris. On the edge of Great Britain the Western Isles are magical, winds and sea swept. That reminds me of this joke:

Auld Queer Goings on in the Western Isles. Told in the Scot's tongue.

Nigel was a great success in the Dot com world but stress was getting him down. He decided with the millions he had made in his work, it was time to retire and lead a more leisurely life.

And so he purchased a But an" Ben, a modern revamped ancient stone dwelling on the most western point of rural Scotland. He settled happily on the Isle of Lewis and marvelled at his decision. Each day he counted in scores the bobbing heads of seals in the bay, saw the spouting of the whale offshore and marvelled at the aerodynamic movements of the eagle as it flew down from its mountain home. One evening the telephone rang. It was the Island's Laird welcoming him to the island and inviting him to a Ceilidh at his castle.

'Do excuse me, but what is a Ceilidh dear Laird?'

'Ah weel, Nigel. It's a sort of a dance, Yes a dance with some music around the log fire. And there's drink, aye I've of got every single malt whisky there is to find on the island. And there's food, oh yes there's lots of food. There's grouse and salmon and anything ye want. And there's sex as well. Oh yes, lots of sex.'

Nigel thought for a moment. All the things in life that he was missing in one evening. It was too good an opportunity to miss – and at the Laird's Castle too.

'Well, I'd be delighted to come to the Ceilidh. But as I've never been to one before, what should I wear? I mean is it formal or not?'

'Oh dinnae bother aboot dressing up', said the Laird. 'There's jist the two of us.'

*

Finally we have not one but three Tesco shops. Two are all night superstores but the nearest is a petrol station and small Tesco shop about a mile from our home. I go there both for shopping at times and getting fuel for the car.

We had run out of porridge. I walked to the store, found a packet of Scott's original oat porridge and took it to the counter. The lady looked up at me.

'Any fuel today, sir?' she asked.

'Yes,' I replied as she checked to see which pump I must have used.

'I had Shreddies this morning but...' I presented my porridge packet to her, 'It will be Scott's Porridge oats tomorrow.'

Bed & Breakfast

'Thank you. I'd like this room for a night. I'll be off by 9.30 tomorrow.'

'Breakfast is from 7.30 to 10am.'

'That's fine. I may be slow to come down. I've got some lumbago.'

'You'll just have porridge like everyone else', she replied.

'Your room is first on the left upstairs. But I must warn you to shut the door at night.'

That seemed an unusual request. 'Why'?

'Well it's our girl. She tends to walk around the house in the middle of the night.'

'Oh , what age is she?'

'Our Sally is 17. She's really sweet, but she does have this problem. So please lock your door.'

The lodger retired to his room wondering just what Sally might look like and why she wandered round the house at night. He imagined her as a buxom teenager flirting with her mother's clientele. Ahaa, he thought. I'm going to leave the door ajar.

Around three o'clock in the morning when he was deep in sleep, Sally quietly entered the bedroom. She saw the lodger sleeping soundly. It was time to surprise him. With one almighty leap, she jumped onto the bed and curled her golden paws under her chin and sighed. Just as the landlady predicted!

*

In an age when couples don't marry but have relationships, it must amaze them that the previous generations remain married all their lives. Well as one who has been married for forty-four years so far, I can tell you it takes some give and take, compromises galore and love. In fact I have a recipé you might enjoy to keep your marriage alive:

This is a response to the charming Sandra A Mushi's entry in AuthorsDen.com. Which do you prefer?

The Good Husband's Guide

Have dinner ready. Plan ahead. Hide the beer tins. Have a good mouth rinse. The night before, make sure you are planning for that delicious meal tomorrow. When you 'phone Meals For Two Express Delivery, make sure it arrives two doors away at your friend Bill's home half an hour before beloved arrives home. Keep Bill in the secret by giving him free football tickets. When the Meals For Two Delivery arrives, make sure all the foil is removed and covertly placed in neighbour's bins. Prepare yourself. Have a shower. Splash on the Tommy liberally.

Remove Girly magazines from settee and replace with the Economist. Turn over a few pages to look as if you have read it. To ensure the rooms are well dusted, open all the windows and hope there will be a good breeze. Be happy to see her. Show you are happy to see her. Show her sincerity in your desire to please her. Place a pack of three by her bedside. When she comes in to change after a hard day's work getting out of her power suit, she will be delighted to see you care. Don't greet her with complaints and problems other than express your disappointment that the store was out of spinach but you managed to get the ingredients for ratatouille en Provence. You really did not mind spending all afternoon cooking. It was too hot outside. Open a new bottle of her favourite red/white wine. Do not let her see the half finished bottle you were drinking in the hammock this afternoon. Oh and...make sure the hammock is back in the store room. Make the evening hers. Line up all the soaps on TV for her this evening. This will give you at least two and a half hours to blog. Let her choose where the annual vacation will be this year. Then return with your ideal holiday booking showing her suggestion was great but it had been brought to your notice by the sales person that it was a particularly beautiful quiet place spoilt by mosquito ponds nearby which the brochure did not show. Make her birthday a special day. Book her on a skydive after telling her it's a short flight over the Grand Canyon. Make sure you wine and dine her at one of your favourite eateries. Remember she is the mistress of the house. (But not during the day). Finally, and this is a bit risky, (especially if she comes across this article)...but...

tell her to log on to AuthorsDen.com …and show her Sandra Mushi's article entitled The GOOD WIFE'S GUIDE. Then with pleading Basset Hound eyes, tell her you are trying to live up to these high expectations… because…she deserves them.

Not often did I hear from a politician, a seminal moment in a country's life. Such an event happened to me in West Africa.

In 1973 on the Akwapim mountain range in Ghana, I met with Daniel Chapman-Nyahu, one of the first politicians in the Government of Kwame Nkrumah, the first black African President and first president of Ghana. The meeting gave a remarkable insight into the formation of a new Republic. I share my recollection of that memorable moment with you.

On the eve of the Gold Coast becoming the Republic of Ghana in 1960, Osagefo Dr. Kwame Nkrumah shared a perplexing problem with Cabinet Minister, Daniel Chapman-Nyahu. Nkrumah instantly dismissed the adjective 'Ghanaian' to describe the citizens of the new Republic. 'The word contains too many 'a's and, 'i's. It will be difficult to spell correctly," he remarked. The two men sought similar familiar examples to solve their problem. 'China – Chinese – Ghanese'? suggested Chapman-Nyahu. 'Then what about Romania – Romanian – Ghanian?" he further suggested. Nkrumah frowned.' Then Cuba – Cuban – Ghanan,' he continued. The President stood up and walked towards the door. He turned to face his Minister.' The people will soon learn to spell and pronounce GHANAIAN.' And so that is how it came about and why we call the delightful people of Ghana today – Ghanaians.

*

I had seen and heard my father pour out weekly sermons. I was used to his literary world. At school there were opportunities to provide essays to mark. But mark was all they did. It was not until I was a student. In part of the course we had to write a story as writing reports would feature in our work. I composed this piece on the train from Edinburgh to Glasgow, one weekend. It did not take long. When I submitted it to my American lecturer, she thought it the best she had ever read. It had made her cry. It was a moving piece of work. She even suggested, I should be an author. That had never been considered as a career, but she had planted a seed in my mind.

Mother's death came suddenly. The family had been a unit of four but now was three – an odd number – and I felt the odd one out. Mother had been always available to oversee my achievements however humble and rectify my regular failings. And she overlooked my mischief too. But her vacuum was felt acutely that morning.

'Well, Michael, you seem to have grown a foot or two since I last saw you,' said an uncle whom I had not seen since I visited him two summers ago at his seaside home in Dorset. His remark meant nothing to me for I was still one of the smallest in the class. I chose not to reply. I simply could not. My silence embarrassed him and with a reassuring pat on my back he moved away.

'Hello Aunt Mae.' I was determined not to remain silent and this aunt had always been most talkative to me in the past. But she too was drained of words. This was not the vital family I had known. Where was the happiness, the laughing? I had never seen such close relatives without smiling faces.

Time broke the barrier which was impeding communication and when the funeral service was over, I sensed some life ebbing back into the house. I poured coffee into cups while relatives talked of their plans for their summer holidays. I just had to break in.

'Uncle, is Milford – on – Sea in England?

This time my question reached its mark.

'That's right Michael. It's in Hampshire not far from Southampton where the Atlantic Liners come in. You would like it there. I'm sure.'

'Oh yes' I replied enthusiastically. Then I thought as I sat with my sister by the fire, what a holiday without mother would be like.

'No, no I don't think I'd like Milford – on Sea.'

'Why ever not?' asked Aunt Mae but all I could bring myself to say was, 'I don't know.'

I felt increasingly secure as the funeral faces of my relatives relaxed into expressions that I knew. Father was more active than usual as he called to announce lunch was ready. He helped Aunt Mae to prepare and serve the meal but I was unaware of the significance of his chores. I still expected Mum to come through the dining room door with the silver plated teapot, but the teapot came without her.

My older sister assumed many of the other roles I had seen my mother perform in the course of a busy day's work but she had not yet acquired the perfection Mum had achieved through her years of service to us and I felt my sister never would. I somehow knew apple pie would never taste the same again nor would breakfast every morning be complete without mother chasing us off to school. Who would do all the things that we accepted only too readily?

Evening came early to the grief stricken house and soon relatives were leaving, returning to continue with their own busy lives. They left as silently as they arrived. When the last car left the drive and mingled with the stream of city bound cars, I was for the first time, aware that I was lonely. This was the beginning of a permanent void.

However, when I returned to the sitting room, I saw not only my father, but within that man, a mother. Qualities I had associated with my mother were indeed visible in him although I had been blind to them before. He caressed my head and patted my back.

'School tomorrow, Michael? Can you make it? A hard lump hit the back of my throat. I looked up at him.

'Yes Dad. I'll go. Let's make the packed lunches.'

*

Now, a cheerier story from the mouths of children.

Childhood recollection misunderstood!

Seven year old Annie gave her 'news' at class news time.

'Last night, Dad pissed on the cat,' she said.

Alarm bells sounded. Was the teacher hearing libidinous, indecent exposure, lewd anti-social behaviour or just what had Annie's father done?.Should Social Services be notified?

The teacher took Annie into the corridor and brought a teacher from another class to have the story corroborated. The teacher asked Annie to repeat her news. Sure enough, she repeated: 'Last night Dad pissed on the cat.'

At 12 noon an emergency Social Services case conference was held.

'Tell me again Annie, what did your Dad do last night?'Annie placed her fists on her waist. 'I told you before, he pissed on the cat.'

The Social Worker sharpened her pencil and made her own enquiry. 'Does he do this regularly?' she asked.

'Oh yes, most nights,' Annie replied. 'You see, we don't let the cat stay outside all night. So Dad opens the back door about 9p.m. and goes Pssssst… Trixy …come in. And she usually does.'

*

A letter which is somewhere now! Another true story.

A good friend in Ghana lost her Father recently. I knew him well in the 1970s when I worked in Tema so I thought I should write to her. The letter had 3 pages so I needed the correct postage stamp to send it to Ghana (from Scotland). I went to a supermarket which has a postal counter. I took the letter with me and placed it in the shopping trolley.

Unfortunately a gust of wind scooped it up as I entered the store and as I looked back, the automatic doors behind me closed. I had to go to the exit and return outside to where the letter would now be found on the ground.

An elderly couple were leaving the store so I could not overtake them or rush round them but when I got through I saw the letter in the hand of a young woman who suffered from Downs Syndrome.

I raised my hand and told her 'It's mine. It's my letter!' She thought it was a game. Before I could reach her, she ran to the post box and posted it!

So to Rosemary in Ghana please accept my apologies if you had to pay for the stamp. I did not know whether to laugh or cry. I guess I did both!

*

INNOCENCE In KIRRIE –
Some memories of a 4 year old, me.

It would take a further year before Hoppy understood the meaning of 'The following ardi inti mations'. Despite hearing this announcement weekly from his father's pulpit, these words were not the speech of daily family talk. "Ardi inti" was reserved for Sunday mornings. Sunday morning was when Hoppy, wearing his best clothes, accompanied his older sister Joan and his mother, took his place in the manse pew.

Intrigued by his middle name 'Hopkins', his earliest efforts to pronounce it caused mirth. So 'opi' became Hoppy and this made him happy as Hoppy sounded like happy and happy was what Hoppy liked to be.

He had become used to his sister leave the manse for primary schooling but he showed no interest in where she had been for most of the day. Instead, Hoppy arranged chairs in rows in the breakfast room to pretend he had a bus to drive to Forfar. He was the ticket collector too and so with guttural grunts, and exaggerated hand manoeuvres, he kept the engine ticking over and the hand brake on while his imaginary passengers paid their fare. An old handbag was strapped over his shoulder providing imaginary change when needed. All this was accompanied by radio music from the crystal set on the chest of drawers by the door. He became familiar with radio theme tunes of the Light programme as he did so.

The sound of Workers Playtime, Listen with Mother and Life with the Lyons but every Saturday night without fail, Hoppy would march up and down the manse hall with a miniature walking stick to the traditional music of Scotland. In the town square he had seen the Pipes and Drums of the massed bands parade in the summer evenings and so he was able to imitate the Drum Major as he held his stick aloft, to the left and to the right. A keen ear had also taught him to bring the stick down on the fourth last beat of the bar. It was a comfortable and unperturbed existence for a four year old.

Hoppy's young life had not however, been without trauma. The cross of Lorraine scar on his stomach, a frequent source of unconscious caressing, was testament to the skills of a Glasgow paediatric surgeon, weeks after Hoopy's birth when pyloric stenosis had been finally diagnosed, as the cause of his fading away. His medical uncle had intervened with the young general practitioner to give a second and wiser opinion. This intervention had certainly benefited Hoppy. There was no evidence of that now. He was really quite chubby. Unbeknown to him, the parishioners knew of his past surgery and it made them occasionally enquire of his heath. He had noticed this was not always asked of his sister. Nor could he detect the nuances of family interaction that had made his grandmother favour his sister as a result of the attention, which he had been given by his parents, during his first weeks of life

Nor had his sister experienced the secret meetings Hoppy had had weekly at the corner shop at the end of the Manse lane while she was at school. It began quite innocently enough when Hoppy stood in front of the shop window nonchalantly eyeing the display of sweet jars.

'And which sort would you like Hoppy?' Miss Fairlie asked.

He could not read the labels. So he selected by colour. 'Um...Ummmm' then he simply pointed at a jar not knowing what it might contain.

Thereupon Miss Fairlie entered the shop with him and bought a small white paper poke of the selected sweets.

'There you are. You know it's not true what they say about Manse sons, is it Hoppy?'

Hoppy did not understand this observation. A smile sufficed as the first sweet entered his mouth. This weekly encounter lasted a full month before suspicions were aroused. But it was not parental discovery.

Sharing the contents of his white paper pokes with his sister strengthened their bond. Being two and a half years younger, left Hoppy in awe of her achievements, in writing, reading and now she even had badges sewn on her brown Brownie tunic.

*

I have had several operations and frankly I can be a bit too relaxed about them whether they are invasive surgery like peritonitis, or cranial nose issues. I've had them all. I'm glad I'm not alarmed about surgery as this farmer was.

Willie was a busy farmer but he had a pain in his side. The doctor sent him to hospital to have a CAT Scan. He was terrified. The nurse explained the procedure.

'Now Willie, it is like lying on a conveyor belt. You simply move along slowly and we have cameras to get to the root of your problem and then we can treat you. It's a pain free procedure. Simply one to diagnose your condition. Nothing to worry about.'

'But I'm really nervous Nurse.'

'Well then, you can play your favourite singing a[...]
Do you have one?'

'Well, in that case I'll have Frank Sinatra.'

The following week Willie lay on the conveyor be[...]
He was ready for the operation. As he started to mo[...]
forward, Frank Sinatra began to sing:

AND NOW, THE END IS NEAR...IT"S TIME
TO FACE THE FINAL CURTAIN...

*

When Life is in perspective, perspective hides from life !

On a warm summer's day in the south of England, two tramps were walking in the countryside. They approached a walled Church wherein lay the graves of many a worshipper. As they approached the gate at the entry of the churchyard, one tramp remarked with some surprise and happiness.

'Gosh, that was a good age!'

His friend asked how old he was.

'162'

'162 ! Who was he?'

'Now let me see, his name is written below. Ah yes, it says MILES from London.'

*

Abbreviations and misunderstandings!

Martha decided to emigrate from the UK to a rural part of Germany and through her e-mail enquired of a

tist.   gent about a suitable small cottage in a
                   ⸝with bathroom ensuite and WC.

                   ⸝an agent was not confident in his
lt.   ⸝d so took a copy of Martha's letter to the
ⁱe   ⸝ English was much better.

               Ahhhh a good church go-er I think. WC can
            ⸝ for a Wesleyan Chapel.

            ⸝d with this information, the Estate Agent
         ⸝o Martha thus:

      ⸝e WC is situated about nine miles from the
   ⸝ence in the centre of a pine forest amid delightful
  ⸝oundings. It is open on a Tuesday and a Thursday.
 ⸝is is unfortunate if you are in the habit of going
⸝gularly, but you will no doubt be glad to hear that a
number of people take their lunch and make a day of it.

The accommodation is good, over eighty seats
and should you be late at any time, there is plenty of
standing room. A bell is rung ten minutes before the
WC is opened. I would specially advise your ladyship to
pay a visit on Tuesdays, as on that day, there is an organ
accompaniment. The volume of sound is excellent, even
the most delicate sound is heard all over the building.

I should be delighted to reserve the best seat for you
and to have the honour to sit next to you. Hymn sheets
are provided, hanging behind the door and the pastor
will come round at intervals to offer any assistance.

Hans Kleen

PS My wife and I have been unable to go for eight
months. This pains us both very much.

13

Life with Books

I have written many books as you will discover and most have a link to my past life. But I should stress, writing books does not make authors wealthy. The book cover, for that is a very important aspect of book-selling, can cost in excess of £450 and the printer and publisher have their cut too. If I sell my books in a shop, they demand 30% of the sales before I have my cut. So, a book selling at £9.99 can leave the author with just over a pound. Imagine having to sell 450 books just to cover the cost of the book cover! So why do I bother to write books? At first it was because I could not find a job after retirement which suited me but I had a story to write. I could only think of Operation Oboe. I did not see the deluge of books I have written now. And they are all in my bookshelf and there they will stay even beyond my years on earth. But I never had thought that two books of my books would be films. And if they are popular, will that lead to a red carpet somewhere, maybe at Nice or Los Angles? Well, you know authors dream, and I do. We may not be able to predict the future but an author's life can be full of surprises.

OPERATION OBOE

I knew my great aunt had married a Hamburg doctor in 1912 and spent time on their honeymoon in Scotland, the following year. I had heard she was also a spy but had no further information about her life. When I retired, this was my first book. Operation Oboe was created from my past in Ghana, the Gold Coast at the time. German missionaries had been taken to the Isle of Man to live out the First World War years and their Presbyterian background led to the first Scottish missionaries taking their pastoral and education posts in The Gold Coast, following the hostilities. It was easy to research the Basel Mission and its importance in Ghana and it led to the intrigue of a Swiss pro German missionary and his undermining the Allied cause. My time in Ghana, the former Gold Coast, inspired me for this book. Years later I gave this book to my uncle, the doctor whose foresight saved my life as a baby, and he

told me he enjoyed reading the story but it was not the real espionage story. He gave me letters from Hilda (not Vera) and more facts about her life and that book came out later as A Reluctant Spy.

PONDERINGS

Operation Oboe had sold well but some elderly readers wondered if it could be reprinted as an enlarged book? So I decided to write a book for those with a need for enhanced words. This book captures some of my stories and poems and is in a larger font. It did not sell particularly well.

Have You Seen My Um….Memory?

Retiring from work with mild cognitive impairment was a shock. I was forgetting to renew warrants, had left the garage pump without paying for fuel and got lost driving in town. No wonder nobody wanted to employ me when they heard that. So I researched my condition of MCI. There is a dastardly direct link. For some MCI is part of the road to Alzheimer's disease. I am only partly down that road but stalling at MCI. I decided to write about the brain, its functioning and its malfunctions, my route to early retirement and a host of aids and tips are provided, be they memory related or simple useful advice. The book was published by Authorsonline then taken up in Denver, given an Americanization of text and printed by Outskirts Press. So my first $ earning book came about.

Poet's Progeny

My father wrote about his link to Robert Burns. He gave me the text and a year later died. The manuscript lay dormant for many a month before I resurrected his story and that of the interlinking generations between Burns and myself. The book was written some ten years after my father's text arrived and I added more of the story to the book. Being a Burns book, sales are good around January but not only in the UK. Burns lovers the world over have heard of this book by word of mouth and it always surprises me when the royalties arrive for this seasonal book.

The Parrot's Tale

The Parrot's Tale tells the story of my African Grey Parrot I had in Tema, Ghana. Kofi was his name and he was the most intelligent of birds. In this book I pretended Kofi escaped and joined the other birds in the sky. This led to 85 yr old Harry to be sectioned after seeking Kofi from the trees near a mental home. This is indeed a comic book with Harry riding on the back of retired policemen John's motorbike. There are many escapades in this 400 page novel and it is seen as one of my best and funniest stories so far.

Review:

A J McNay *5.0 out of 5 stars* The Parrot's Tale. A feel good novel with lots of twists.

The story links a extremely clever parrot, motorbike, two main characters and numerous areas of Scotland in an entwining tale. It is one of those books once you start reading, it's impossible to lay down.

The Crazy Psychologist.

Our daughter, Laura, who is a clinical psychologist, told me one Christmas of her unusual colleague who led a double life. I found her story interesting and said it could make a good book. You should have seen my daughter's expression. Her anxiety subsided when I told her I would chose another name and set the book sufficiently far away on Orkney, where I have some relatives. I went to Orkney and sold the book on the island of Rousay at the harbour shop.

TAKE THE LEAD

This is a book about all the dogs in my life from Kirriemuir, Glasgow, Tema, London, Troon, Pakistan and Dumfries. Some deserved to be put down and one in particular bit the teacher who belted me. Ah yes, that story is in this book. But by far the other dogs enhanced their owner's life. Each breed has its own personality as every dog-owner tells you or you will discover. But two weeks looking after a Basset hound was the most tiresome chore. I would shout from the bottom of the staircase to my wife to say that the salad was on the table and my wife would come down from where she was working. As we entered the dining room, the plates were as clean as a whistle, and the Basset hound looking as pleased and satisfied as he could be.(We had been looking after my brother's hound when they were on holiday) Our black Labrador Czar was a similar food consumer extraordinary but with collies it's entirely the other way. A full plate of meal and even a bit of salmon or chicken on top interests Georgie as it did Tâche but they linger for minutes before consumption. Sometimes for much longer. I should learn from collies and not rush my own meals.

I have written three children's books and already referred to Chaz the friendly Crocodile. So to book number 2.

Lawrence the Lion Seeks Work was the next children's book. All of a sudden it seemed circuses lost their animals. Only grandparents can inform a new generation how a cage was erected and lions or tigers entered the circus arenas and obeyed the master's whip. The question on my mind was to wonder what had happened to those friendly circus animals once they were barred from the circus. So Lawrence the lion goes in search of work and eventually his quest is resolved and he finds work which suits a lion in the community. There is also a Dutch version of Lawrence the Lion Seeks Work (Laurence de Leeuw op zoek naar werk)

The final children's book, **Danny the Spotless Dalmatian,** came about through my mother. I came across a picture of my 12 year old mother with her family pet, a Dalmatian. I forget its name. Researching Dalmatians I discovered that they are born with no spots. The spots appeared around four weeks. So, my mind tackled the question; if a Dalmatian had no spots was it a Dalmatian, an unhappy Dalmatian perhaps? He needed spots and so the search for spots began and they appeared everywhere. On frocks, when in a difficult spot, on dice, of milk, I think you get the idea. But, of course, Danny did find spots and they could appear when he wanted. He became a very special Dalmatian.

DANNY
the spotless dalmatian

written by
MILLER CALDWELL
Illustrations by Katy Dynes

7 Point 7 on the Richter Scale

In 2006 I was in Pakistan managing the camp at Mundihar, following the S.E. Asian Earthquake. I have already told you how that came about. Each night I filled a page of my diary, recalling my activities of the day. On my return home,

I published my diary of my time in the North West Frontier Province and went to Glasgow and filled the shelves of some Pakistani shops. All 800 book proceeds went to Muslim Hands.

Restless Waves

This book was the result of having been the writer in residence in Prison. From the confines of prison cells, I set off on a world cruise as the boat's writer afloat, in this book. Armed with brochures and maps by my side, the book set sail. I have never had a recreational cruise, myself, sailing from Tema to Rotterdam coming back from Africa was no cruise. In Restless Waves are hair raising confessions, drug smuggling and more gentle activities on board and on shore involving the writer and as you can imagine meals were sumptuous and entertainments numerous and varied. This was a fun book to write. One reviewer wrote: "With a touch of Agatha Christie in each event, Miller Caldwell introduces diversity in his novel Restless Waves, taking us on a world cruise. Each new port and country brings us local knowledge and colour. A travelogue; a story and certainly an intriguing insight into life on a cruise ship. A highly recommended read!"

Jim's Retiring Collection.

During his last calling at Glenfarg, an elder who was an amateur artist, heard of some of my father's amusing stories and provided him on his retirement, with a selection of cartoons. Each cartoon is accompanied with a biblical text and a commentary to bring the passage into the 21 century. Here are three of the cartoons. You can add your own captions. The captions are the real ones.

Dad had two services to take on Sundays. First at Glenfarg and almost one and half hours later, after a coffee, at Abernethy. Sometimes he did not quite make it to the vestry. The caption reads: "I to the Hills will lift mine eyes."

A bride enters the vestry for the first time and sees the Communion Cup in the glass bookcase. She exclaims: 'Mr Caldwell, I didna ken you wis an athlete!"

A farmer died and his last will and testament required him to have his ashes scattered in the field by the farmhouse. As the service progressed three bulls approached. My father kept one eye open. The beasts then bowed their heads as the funeral ceremony proceeded. It was noted that it was a "Mooooving experience."

JIM'S RETIRING COLLECTION

Miller Caldwell

Miss Martha Douglas

My mother's uncle was a press photographer with the Daily Sketch, a London based national newspaper. It's final edition was in 1971. He died in 1916. He left some period photos which I have inherited. Here are some.

Press photographer David Harvie.

A suffragette is arrested.

King George V rides out.

A State Funeral of George 1 of Greece of the Hellenes.

Queen Mary and King George arrive at the theatre.

Mrs Alice Keppel was a mistress of King Edward VII

Field Marshall Frederick Sleigh Roberts VC, KS, KP, GCB, OM, GCSI, VD, PC, FRSGS aka 'Bobs'. Sept 30th 1832-November 14th 1914. A proponent of World War 1.

King George V on a Surrey street.

From these photos, I created the protagonist Martha Douglas, a nurse who fell out with her Glasgow hospital matron and moved to London. She was imprisoned as a suffragette but released to serve in the Queen Alexandra's Royal Army Nursing corps at the front in France, where she tended wounded soldiers.

As the war drew to a close her feelings for a partially blinded New Zealand soldier led to romance.

Yet as I wrote this book, my mind was fixed on the brave soldiers in Kirriemuir whose medals were many and well earned as they strolled about in the wee red town. I imagined them on the front at Passchendaele, preparing for the onslaught of death.

A Clerical Murder

A Clerical Murder is part of two books in one, the other being The Trials of Sally Dunning. The psychiatrist finds his caseload comprises of several clerics. He decided some group work seems in order. But fault lines appear and one cleric is murdered, by, well that would be telling!

The Trials of Sally Dunning

A close neighbour with autism has had a troubled life. I thought that a good plot but changed the sex and location to Wigan, a town I know well. She comes up trumps in the end with a very happy ending.

Untied Laces

Ten years ago I wrote my autobiography. Eleven years later these are my memories. My autobiography was a linear story. This memoire dips into my life at different stages. Two different books about the same author.

Dementia Adventure

The protagonist is a retired postman on Arran at Blackwaterfoot. He maintains his early walks and sees some foul play. Police do not believe him as he has dementia but he calls wolf once too often. Wasting police time is seen as a serious matter by the Sheriff on the bench but did he see anything untoward at all. And if so can it be proved?

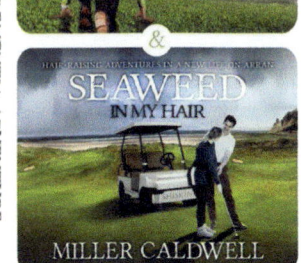

Seaweed in Her Hair with Dementia Adventure Murders at Blackwaterfoot

A bull unearths a hand in a field and a murder enquiry is underway. With no missing persons on the island, the case grows cold. PC Rory Murdoch and his commanding officer on the mainland don't get on. Rory is widowed with a handicapped daughter Ella. He is dismissed from the police service for not making progress but Rory received a call from Belgium and the case is solved. He is reinstated and his boss demoted and sent to Jura. Two unrelated deaths occur and they too are murders but Rory finds the killers while his daughter is flown to Glasgow's Victoria hospital. Ella dies. He is comforted by a near neighbour whose affections come Rory's way. I think I'll stop there.

A Lingering Crime

I have already told the story of this book, the circumstantial evidence of sexual abuse and the film rights obtained. This is the book's cover.

The Reluctant Spy

Written ten years after Operation Oboe, The Reluctant Spy, complete with historical documents tells the real story of Hilda Campbell. She was also Hilda Richter, wife of a Hamburg doctor and eventually Lady Hilda Simpson, wife of the British Ambassador to Finland. In between her double agent status brought MI 5 and the Nazi war machine to bear on her but she never faulted despite a son in the Hitler Youth movement. One of the last true stories to come out of World War 2.

Caught in a Cold War Trap.

Well was I a Russian Spy? I asked that question in an earlier chapter. This is the book and by the time this book is published will be further along the path leading to a film. The Russian embassies have a lot to come clean about.

Betrayed in the Nith

This book became very popular in Dumfries and its library. Almost certainly because it featured the river

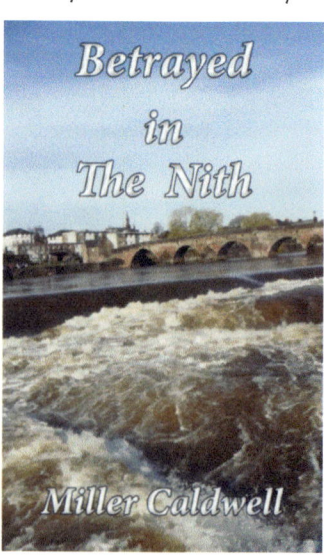

Nith. It's the story of a handicapped man who is cared for by a number of well-wishers but he is drowned in the Nith. Were his friends responsible or someone you might have least expected?

The Last Shepherd began when I had a visitor at my front door. Jim Ramsay is a Stewartry farmer and was sent by the Dumfries Arts centre, at Gracefield, who had suggested he see me. He wanted a film script of the book. I told him films are very difficult to secure but I'd write the book. Little did I realise the power of advertisement in the Farmer's Weekly magazine

and his farming community. The story is about the clash of cultures when a family from the south of England holiday in the farming community in the Stewartry of Kirkcudbrightshire. An ex-marine benefactor is good with a rifle and uses it to bring order but does not survive his injuries. We learn about farming life and the loyalties which it creates.

The Clown Prosecutor

Sam Harvie, son of a circus manager becomes a court prosecutor. However his antics in

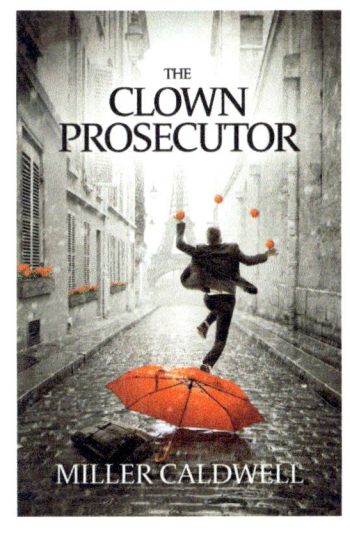

court get him sacked. He tries three other jobs but in hilarious scenes he is sacked from each one. He has a holiday in France where he meets the English correspondent of Le Figaro. They fall in love. In Paris he spends a night in a Parisian lift but eventually finds contentment in Paris. This is the funniest book I have written.

14

Two Charity Books

A Dream Net

With a magnifying glass perhaps, you will see that contributions come from all over the word. We all dream, usually we are nocturnal dreamers but some are day dreamer too. After all many are authors! From a covid ward in Siberia, to Kyrgyzstan and Romania, Australia and many parts of the UK and America, this net was cast far and wide to bring you a unique book to raise money for Alzheimer's Research. Please buy a copy and support Alzheimer's Research. Clink Street are the publishers.

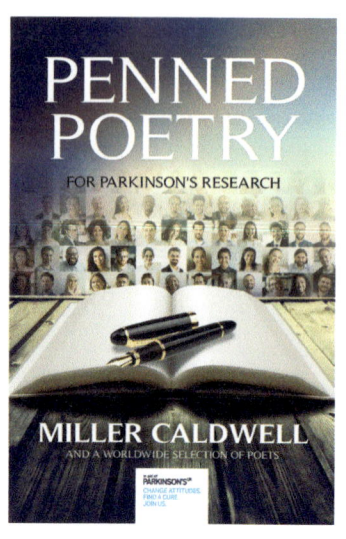

Penned Poets for Parkinson's Research

Also a charity book, this time for Parkinson's Disease, is **Penned Poets for Parkinson's Research**. Again contributing and award winning poets come from far afield and the poetry is varied in style and theme. An ideal book to take to bed and select a poem for you to dream about! City Stone Publishing are the publishers.

Please purchase your copy and support Parkinson's Research.

Finally a book commissioned by the NHS. An end – of –life book. This came about by a dog walk. I walked a black Labrador called Bobby, its owner was a police woman. Her cousin passed by one day and discovered I was an author. She is a health lecturer. She asked me to the college to talk about my MCI. Then she proposed I write an end of life booklet. The result was **It's Me Honest It Is.** It has various sections in which to write about friends and family, likes and dislikes wishes and fears. These are important discussions when in the final stages of life. The booklet is laid by a hospital bedside and the professional attending can see and read about the patients likes, dislikes, favourite author, food, holiday etc

etc. Finally there is a page to record final wishes. A burial or cremation perhaps? If so, where should the ashes be cast? Valuable information for family members afraid to ask difficult questions.

15

My Writing Life

There are poets and there are authors. And never the twain shall meet. No, not quite like that. Authors take a break and sometimes write poems. Poets never stop writing poetry. Each genre has its own demands and I can't say I am a real poet but I give you some of my more popular offerings.

I purchased Writing Poetry by John Whitworth and one of his exercises was to read Hiawatha, note its rhythm (trochaic tetrameter) and then write about some daily activity. I chose to make soup!

SOUP FOR HIAWATHA

Boil the water in the kettle, empty it into a pot
Cut the garlic and the onion, wash the lentils quite a lot.
Slice the squash and leek and onion
Cry with tears of happiness.
Carrot, garlic, red potato, bay leaf, pepper but no salt.

See the froth fall and rise, from the gathering in the pot
Skim the froth into a cup, careful now, for it is hot
Lower heat and make a coffee, listen to the radio.
Sing along if you know it, add a cube of chicken stock.
Squeeze tomato purée gently, stir with vigour, lower heat.

Open wide the kitchen window, hear the sounds of cars
compete.

Twenty minutes after cooking, liquidise the soup you've
made
Smell aromas most inspiring, wash the ladle and the pot.
Add a knob of salt less butter, let it cool, and go to shop.

See the tins in Tesco sitting, instant that and instant this
Stock again the main ingredients, chat to friends, you've
really missed.
They will see you've cut your finger, lift it up and then
explain
Cutting garlic isn't easy, sharp the blade and sharp the
pain.

Then for tea-time, set the table, fork and knife and
pudding spoon
Taking pride of place beside them sit the bulbous soup
spoon doon!
Set a place-mat and a coaster on to which cold water place
Serve the soup then with eyes closed, bow your head,
and say the Grace

By the shore of River Nith. By the shining Solway Sea
Works an author making soup, this writing block made
    recipe.
Spring each year brings a promise from nature. This
poem is my example.

April's Promise

Early warmth with rays of sun
First cut of the lawn
Forsythia and the daffodil
Brighter early morn
Easter promise once again
Chocolate eggs galore
Showers of hail then rain then sun
But winter is no more

All to do in April month
Last rounds of the Cup
Lambing over for the year
Quite big, the Christmas pup

April banish all our dreads
Our failings and our fears
Remove the doubt and cobwebs
And all those salty tears
Enjoy the new life in the land
Returning birds and flowers
Our hopes for brighter days to come
Under budding bowers.

For several years it was my duty to take my daughter for riding lessons. While sitting in the car as the riders set off on a trek, the pen met my pad.

The Riding Lesson

Sentinel firs stained by the fumes of urban exhaust
await torrential rain to bathe each herringbone
pine and disturb the secretive bullfinch from its
enveloping cover.

Stone walls crafted by skill and care
ride the contours of hills herding aimless sheep,
accommodating miniature fauna
hiding them from the keen eyed hawk.

Bobbing heads of trotting riders shake equine
bones beneath
saddle, reins of leather, metal bit between the teeth.

Such are the sights of the hour in which a father
sits, aware of the fading car battery as love songs
enter his thoughts.
This is the hour each week father brings his
daughter to riding lessons.
A weekly homage of tranquillity in all seasons.
To see the age old harmony of rider and horse
Where a gentle kind of love is shared.

*

I have always loved dogs. When 'between' dogs, I have walked the dogs of the infirm. This poem was about one such dog's life. A Poem to honour the dogs in our lives.

A Best Friend

She walked her dog though stooped by old age
Her eyesight was fading removed from each page

No matter the weather each day without fail
In sun and in rain, in snow and in hail
Prince was led on his lead through the park
By the river sometimes but never when dark.

We met now and then through the medium of dogs
Without them I doubt if we'd exchange many words
I learned that she taught many years in the town
And remembered the pupils now they had all grown

Now in her nineties life was beginning to ebb
Both her and on Prince, caught in its web.
No walks no lead no dog now to see
The ambulance came to her home around three.

The sirens were loud and the lights flashing blue
The mourners formed an orderly queue.

I still walk my dog but I noticed last week
That Prince was enjoying some hide and some seek

A young lad was throwing his ball to and fro
Prince knew at once where to run and to go

Then I thought for a moment on what I was seeing
A change of pace, of trust and of being

What a Best Friend really is.

A holiday in Italy inspired this poem. On 1st September
the deck chairs had been stored, schools had resumed
and the holiday period was over for Italians but not us.

ITALY in SEPTEMBER

A velvet green canopy over a collar of basalt rock
protects the dry crisp plain beneath
nibbled by the ink-blue Mediterranean Sea.

Italy in September relaxes after the annual
summer assault of heat, of visitors and of cars.

Deep in the countryside, where silence glimpses
the afterlife, the stain of voices emerge greeting,
shuffling on sun baked grit.

The day is announced. The dancing horizon is
penetrated by hydro pylons bringing energy to
fuel the day in the kitchen and homes
of a people known only by their smiles.

Descendants of Greek invaders or Roman
Legionnaires, they roam no more, content in
sharing their harmony with nature, and sun
seeking northern visitors.

Night falling rain stirs dreams of an orchestra of
dripping leaves, splashing paths and roof tops
performing an impromptu drum roll.

But in the morning a calm atmosphere prevails
with the occasional drip left to descend and make
its way by branch and leaf to the vegetation beneath.

Grey clouds protect the land from a dying
September sun, conserving a sharp hot moment of
penetration when least expected.

Then, and only then, swim naked in the enclosed
bay surrounded by cliffs and caves where tax free
profiteering once flourished to the sway of the
cutlass and eye patch of the Adriatic sea dog.

But now a haven, to refresh tired limbs
and repel the rays of sun striving to burn each
pigment of exposed skin.

Feet tread wearily on sharp moving grit.
The nude torso fights to gain balance on land
once more while shedding sea salt drips in eyes
and to the dry shore
leaving footprints of a moment in time.

Scent the rosemary and mint in flared nostrils
recalling servings of hot roast lamb,
while seeing the very same beasts roaming
the Amalfi hills oblivious to their future, and me to
    mine.

Down the Drain

Beneath the colourless heavy skies
Is a land awaiting the downfall?
To cleanse the parched soil
To satisfy flora and fauna?
While in the home the kettle boils with rapidity
The tea is sipped dignifiedly gripped by two strong
    fingers
While the pinkie retreats fearing the heat of the cup.
The bath water is run with force into the bubbly studs
I enter and let the suds seek crevices, nooks and
    crannies.
I lie back contemplating the source of this cleansing
    activity
And when the temperature lowers, the foot engages
    the plug.
The teapot is emptied and the toothpaste swirls away
They all assemble, Down the Drain.

A baby chimp comes to Scotland

Oh daisy sweet daisy
How yellow you are
Not known in the jungle
My home, now so far.
They say I'm almost human
But my manners are well bred
I do not steal or fight
As many humans do instead.
You say you all like me
That's not easy to believe
So why the guns that killed my Mum
And made me have to leave?

When I was in Pakistan, we played cricket. Both sides vied for me to be in their team. Depite my pleading that I was Scottish, they still wanted me to play. Out first ball. Oh you were not ready. Out second ball. Doubts raised.

Perhaps Miller is a bowler and they all nodded their agreement. First ball...WIDE second ball...WIDE. Doubts if I really was from the UK. I again explained we don't play cricket in Scotland. Having said that, in Dumfries we have a fairly good cricket team. The team consists of a New Zealander by a few ex-public school Scots and the others are English or from the former British colonies.

Not everyone plays cricket. Only the English colonialists introduced it to the Commonwealth.

Green grass lovingly combed every other day
Pitch perfect, is the verdict, the players often say.
A hard core leather ball hurtles down the balding wicket
The batsman's heart skips a beat before he decides to hit it.
Has it gone far enough, beyond the fielders grasp?
Will it reach the boundary under a thorny rasp?
Can it be retrieved and thrown back into play?

Will the runner be out, or safely home without delay.
See the anguished bowler try to bamboozle with his throw
The umpire checks his feet, have they crossed the line below?
Over half the team are out of sight beyond the playing
*   ground*
For the others are in, till those are out, I think that's
*   what I've found.*
At times the ball is hit high into the sky-blue air
A cry of calls descend, and point up in despair
The fielder catches briefly then throws the ball up high
The umpire then decides, he must not tell a lie.

On warm shores far away they play all round the clock
In England it's played seriously, and the papers make
*   them talk*
It matters much to know which County wins the league
And which club goes the course despite suffering fatigue.
But now I must reveal the picture on display
It was taken in Dumfries where a group of them
*   sometimes play*
So I wonder if the game will take an interest abroad
Or maybe best discovered, in poetry's every word.

Only those who know the Collie…

Old bows to young recalling his puppyhood
Young bows to old respecting authority
Together they communicate silently
Wishing to possess what each other has not
Cousins in nature, living far apart

They meet irregularly but recognise
The breed of the Border Collie
Faithful, obedient and sometimes friendly
Aloof, alert, awaiting instructions
Servant and companion roles perfected
Awaiting my instruction or call to dinner
A satisfaction for man and his dog.

Finally, a universal declaration of love.

The Magic of Love

Toes on carpet creeping softly towards the covers
Of the harbour which protects the tired body till
*   dawn*
Nail boots on the carpet will announce the new day
Sonorous sleep and dreams are all but gone.

Spikes upon the green velvet putting place
Golfers getting ready to hit that ball to outer space
Slippers on for evening yours to sit and contemplate
Then switch off all lighting and retire to that secret
*   place*

Bare feet in the bed and all that nature brought
A touch, a confirmation. Two bodies intertwine
Then as one, the movement gains momentum
And the love that's yours has now become mine.

16

Time to Take My Leave

I cannot write about tomorrow. I find I live for each day. Yes, I plan some dates in my diary and I see a double 70th birthday celebration in Sussex in the first week of May is looming. I can't face a drive as far south so we'll drive to Wigan and train our way down to London and then proceed to Sussex. Jocelyn plans that we meet more friends down there, a long lost South African relative encounter too as well as a visit to my sister. I think we will be gone a week. Georgie will resume his life with good friends Bill and Karen while we are away. On reflection, after an AA Route Map inspection, we will be passing London with a wide berth. So, I have decided to drive down after all. Life is like that sometimes. Decision made then decision altered a few days later. I told Jocelyn not to give a brief case to charity one day and two days later I agreed. Seems I need a moment of reflection and I suppose I should not be so adamant in the first place.

Autumn Voices, in which I serve on their steering committee, is a web-present organisation encouraging the elderly (over 60s in fact) to engage in poetry, writing, playing instruments and generally being supported to be active in their latter years in communities around Scotland. Competitions are also set by Autumn Voices.

Thanks to Covid, I have been the longest serving President of the Dumfries Burns Club, from 2019-2022. The AGM later this month, will determine what role I may retain in our committee, other than past president.

I played golf a couple of years ago on Arran at the Shiskine's 12 hole course. I admit I had a few lucky no, really good shots, around the pin but my swing has swung and as I see the clubs in the garage, I begin to wonder who might make better use them. With arthritis in the left leg and Parkinson's in the right hand, it's time to strike golf off the list of sports I have enjoyed playing.

Strangely I remain the press secretary of the Dumfries Probus Club. (Professional Business persons club.) I don't think members know how much of a challenge that is for me. I take notes of every guest speaker's talk, then send the script to the Dumfries Standard every two weeks. In fact, it's a fairly short sighted club. The average age being in the upper eighties crawls ever onward and upward with no new younger members joining. It was felt a move to encourage women to join might solve the problem of dwindling numbers but the first female Probus member has yet to make an appearance. At this rate the club is likely to fade away before too long. That is not an uncommon feature of clubs in the 2020s. Such clubs as the Dumfries Burns Club and Probus had their heyday in the fifties and sixties when television was a one or two channel entertainment source. Now with political correctness gone a little too far in my humble opinion, also in the mix, multi media channels and Netflix, not to mention the ubiquitous cell phones which record the users every waking moment, commitment to clubs offers little interest these days, especially in taking on committee roles.

In the musical smash hit HAMILTON is the line: *Will they tell my story? Whether my story will be told, I'll never know but it can be read.* That about sums up the works of any author. A copy of each of my books sits at the top of the stairs in a glass bookcase. When I am no longer here and our girls are left with the chores clearing the house, the bookcase will have had its day but what of my shelves of books? I wonder what will happen to them. Perhaps they will find a place on the table at Tesco or perhaps recycled in a paper skip. That may be their final destination but some remain on Amazon and every now and then a sale occurs. I recall my uncle David, who was a vet at Thornhill. After his death he received his largest Premium Bond winning. Perhaps a third book will become a film. That should create a smile for my family, as a cheque comes into the estate of the late Miller Caldwell.

But late is not one of my faults. I tend to be there on time, if not in excessively good time. Jocelyn on the other hand, is the risk taker of the family. Yet on only one occasion did she miss the train to Wigan but we went to Lockerbie only to find another train had been put on from Glasgow, so she did not have to wait very long and that train did not necessitate a change at Carlisle.

Joce usually comes up trumps. But I came up trumps in marrying her.

And that seems an appropriate way to end this book. But not just yet! I end with a poem. A poem about Parkinson's disease. This condition may result in this book being my last. It was written especially for Parkinson's day, by my friend Joe McGurk, the new poet in residence at the Dumfries Burns Club.

Parkinson's Awareness

It's oh so sure
I pray struggles gone
No known cure
From disease many suffer from
Move at pace with the placement
Stun, demanding
Coming from a shaky foundation
Understanding
We exactly need
The heart is to say
For that we plead
On Parkinson's Day
I may move slow
That is a cost
Help me sooth though
Balance is lost
Not to dwell
Deep and scarred
Anosmia loss of smell

Sleeping's hard
Be in my body, it's rough
We are to quote
See oddly enough
I'm easily approached

It's not so rare
Why cage it?
Don't be scared
There are five stages
A day smiled
Scale it this with pleas
The first stage is mild
Won't interfere with daily activities
Then blur
It'll amaze you
Tremor
Rigid is stage two
Not to discard
Pen the way it's to be
Walking is hard
Then for stage three
Yes it's depleting
Proving it, oh
Hard dressing and eating
Movements are slow
Then it exhausts
Gaze more
Independence is lost
In stage 4

Through the state
With this
Stage 5 hallucinate
Stiffness
It's real there
This it has led
To a wheelchair
Or forbidden to bed
Time shows the hills
Show it to say
Fine Motor skills
Are going away
What to do?
See there's a lot to be
Here – talk it through
Please talk to me…

Goonae no dae that?

Mind ya, I'm glad ye did.

17

CREDITS

Spiffing Covers provide this book's cover as they have done so with almost all of my books. To **Stefan**, in particular, he has the insight and drive to get into the author's mind and deliver stunning results. What a wonderful friend.

M J Steel Collins is my supportive editor and founder of Beul Aithris, my publishers. She is patient with my demands. Too many I admit. But I'd be lost without her.

The Society of Authors have been a solid rock for me since my Parkinson's disease appeared. I am now on the Society of Authors Disability and Chronic Illnesses zoom group and of course the Society vet my contracts too.

Alan, Stuart, Margaret and Joyce, are my supportive local team, who once were all keen badminton players in D&G but now Tai Chi, golf, David Livingstone Guide and CAB keep their minds and bodies fit.

Alan Collins is a good Lockerbie friend who sheds his eyes over my work and gives constructive encouragement.

Bill and Karen Shankland are dog lovers. In particular, with the collie breed. That suits Georgie and we are most fortunate in that our occasional excursions far afield do not clash with Bill and Karen's travels. So was it dogs that brought us together? No, the classrooms and sports fields at Anniesland in the 1960s is where Bill and I studied and played rugby, many years ago.

Eunice and Robert McDonald are excellent neighbours and we rely on each other increasingly to get chores done, sort out difficulties and keep abreast in world affairs.

Cyril Barnett is my Wigan friend, reviewer of my books, dog lover and all round sound advisor.

Moira Weatherall and **Joe McGurk** bring their youthfulness to the Dumfries Burns Club. Moira as the new Secretary and Joe, as the poet in residence of the club.

Taps-Aff (Scots Vernacular) Literally 'tops off.' The removing of one's shirt in the event of warm weather. Now an expression describing good times being had.
Taps-Oan, the Antonym: Literally 'tops on' Now an expression describing inclement weather or being down on one's luck.

The successes and pitfalls of an author's life frequently stem from his activities. Miller has brought an interesting Head of State to tears and confronted the world's most wanted man; fled the UK to gain sanity and found a wife in darkest Africa. A school failure but a post graduate scholar. Such are the Taps aff and Taps oan situations which colour my life and as a consequence, my books.